CARTOONS BY
LAF

EGGBERT'S DIARY
FOR EXPECTANT MOMS

EGGBERT AND EGGBERTA

A brand new edition
in the form of a diary

Printed with permission

Compiled by Judi Quelland

With gratitude to Susie Barker Lavenson,
Daughter of Percy Barker, the original publisher.

Original cartoons by LAF
Lester A. Friedman

Copyright © 2010

All rights reserved. No part of this book may be used or reproduced in any
manner whatsoever without written permission.
Published 2010 using the material from the original Eggbert books.

Printed in the United States of America.

Eggbert is here again. Well, not quite here – but he'll be born soon. Meanwhile, he is developing and refining his definite and often unique ideas on love and life, digestion and indigestion, sex and even sisters. And Sis is wide-eyed with wonder at his wit and wisdom.

Whether you are expecting your own little one, or just expecting to laugh, Eggbert and Eggberta will not disappoint you.

Eggbert and this diary will take the expectant Mom on a wondrous journey through morning sickness and doctors appointments to that amazing moment when she first felt life inside her; and sonograms and baby showers and preparing the nursery. In this diary she will record all that she is feeling, and doing and thinking about the up-coming changes in her life. Years from now this personal record of her pregnancy will bring back all the wonderful, funny and surprising memories of this very blessed event. We wish all Moms love, joy, fulfillment, and we provide this diary as forever proof that humor is the best medicine in the world.

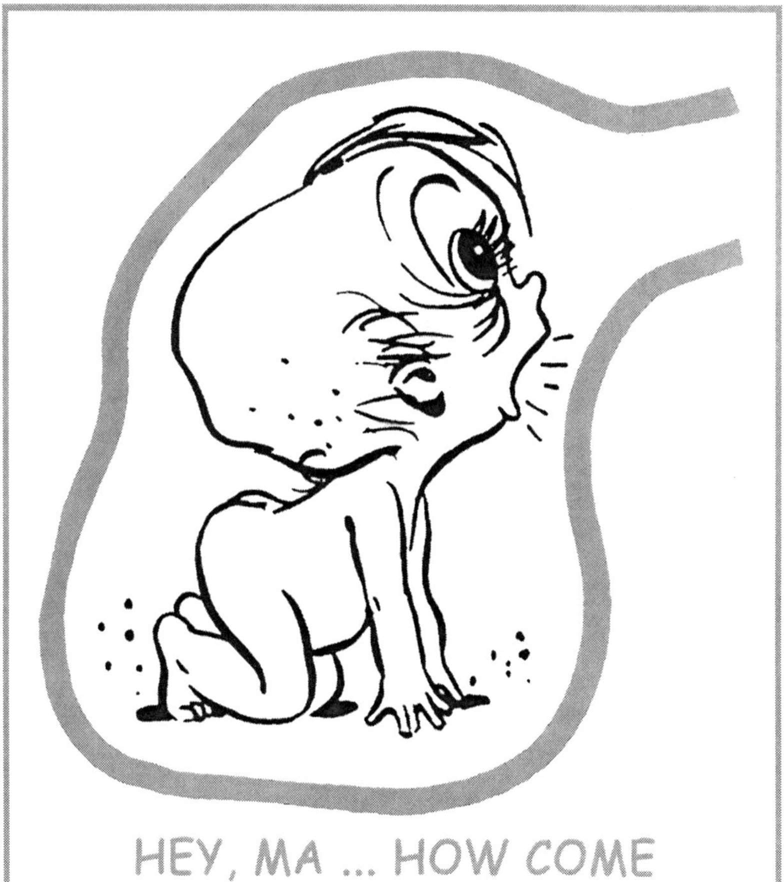
HEY, MA ... HOW COME
I'M DOWN HERE, HUH ?

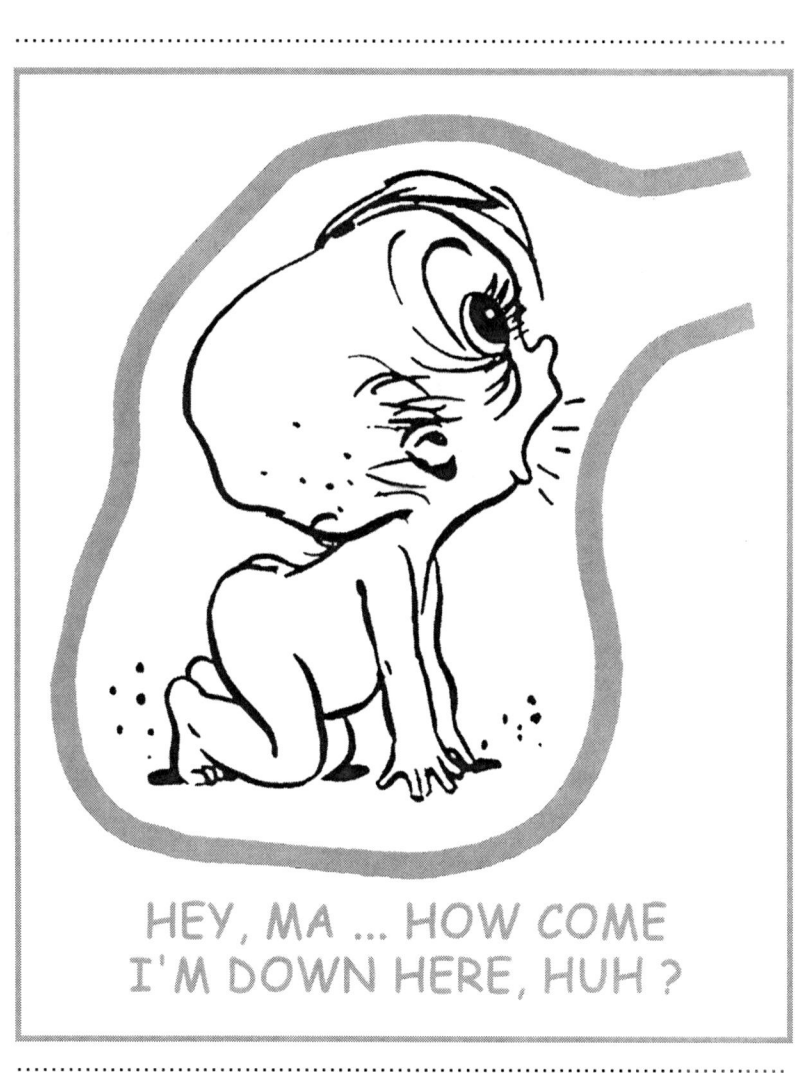

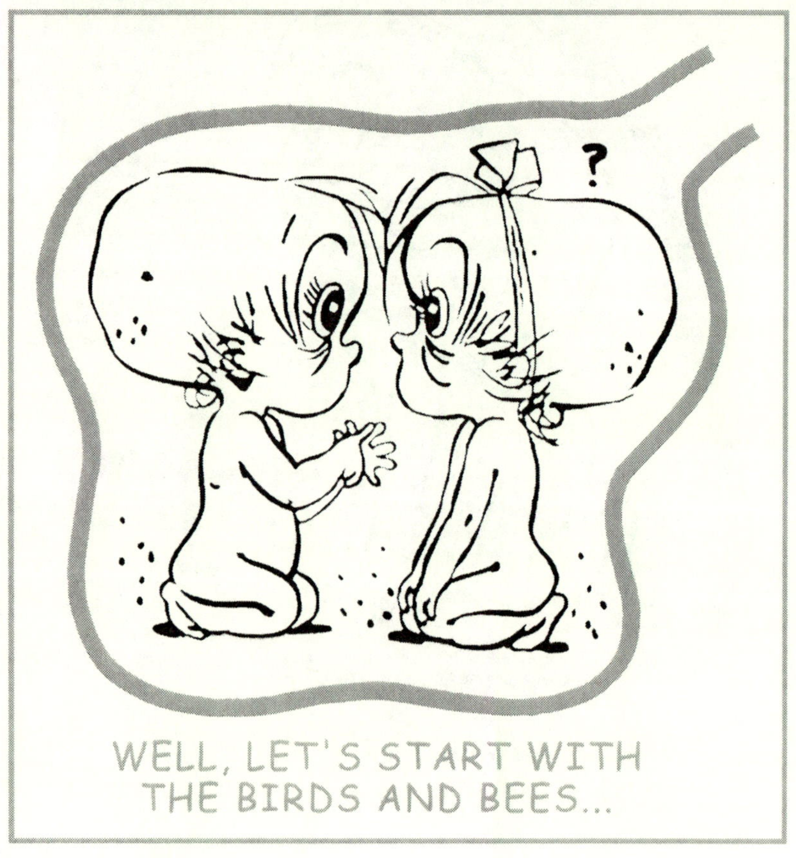
?

WELL, LET'S START WITH
THE BIRDS AND BEES...

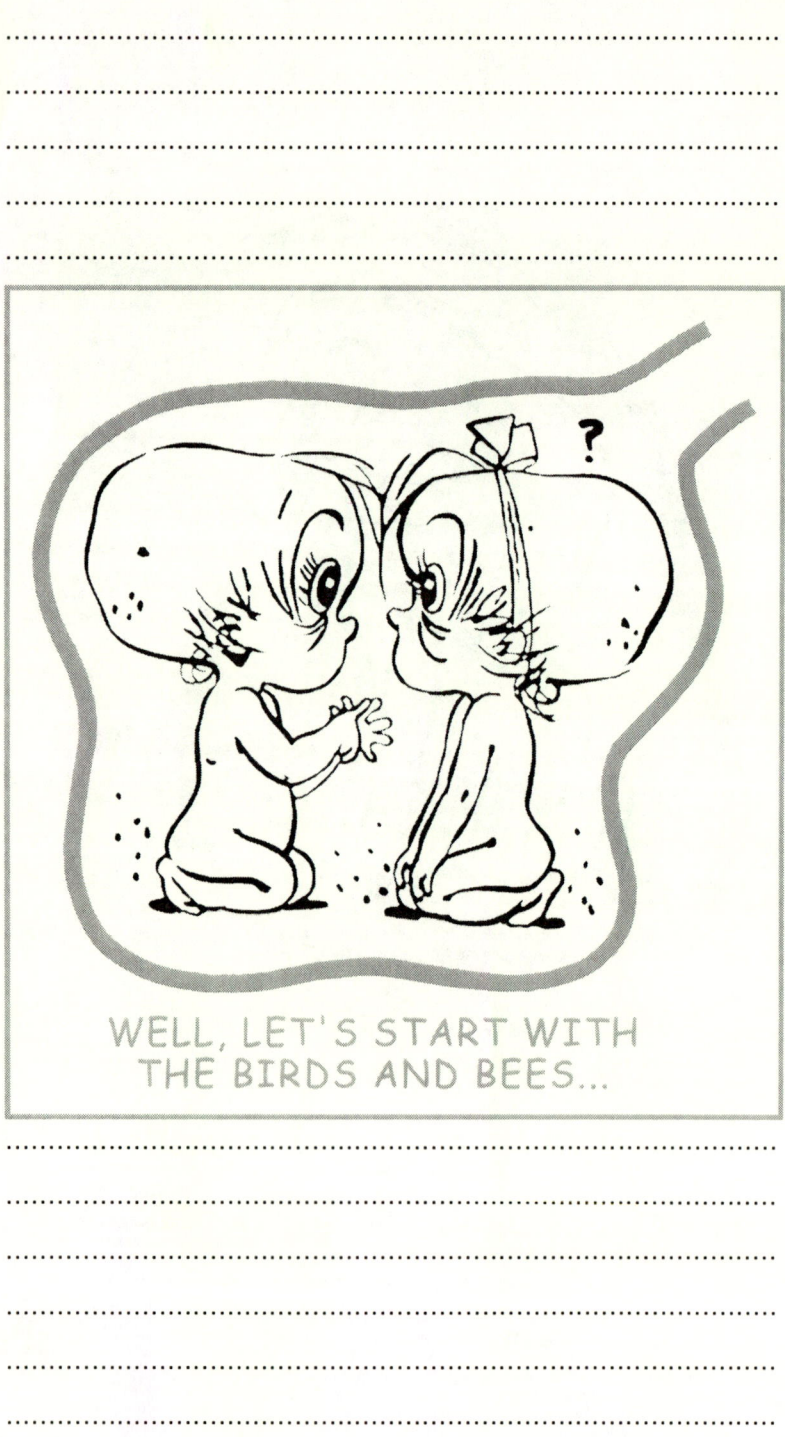

A Little About Your Mom:

....
....
....
....
....
....
....
....
....
....
....
....
....
....

And Some About Your Pop:

....
....
....
....
....
....
....
....
....
....

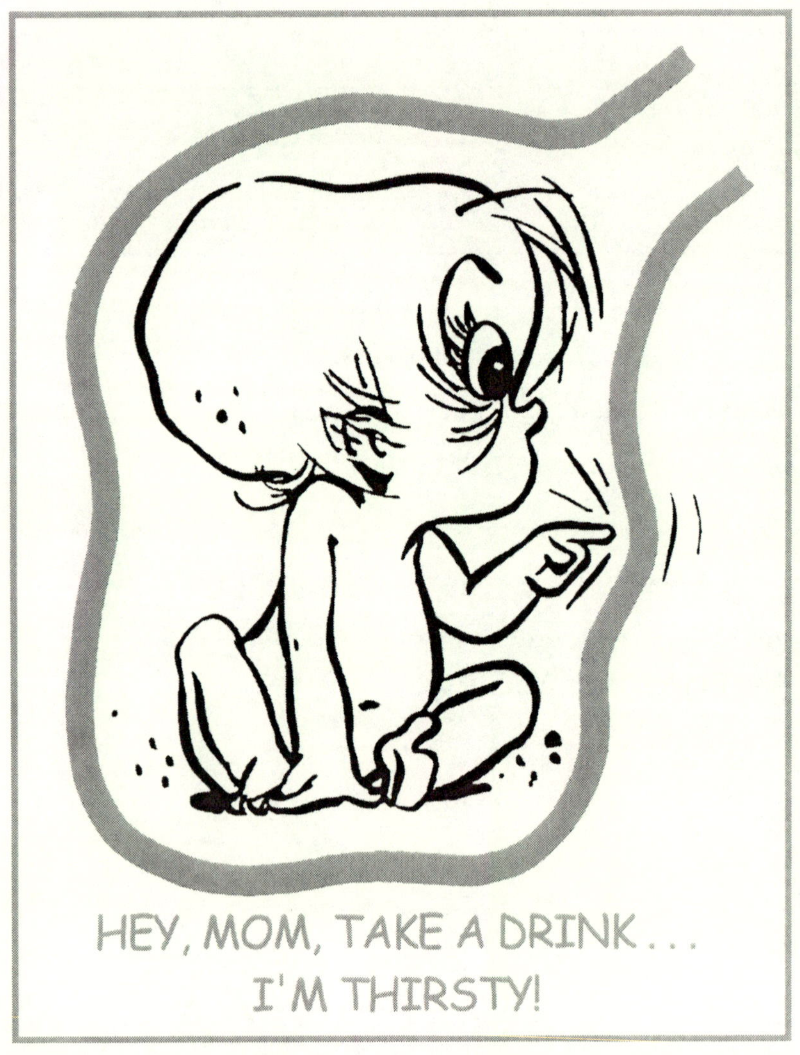

HEY, MOM, TAKE A DRINK . . .
I'M THIRSTY!

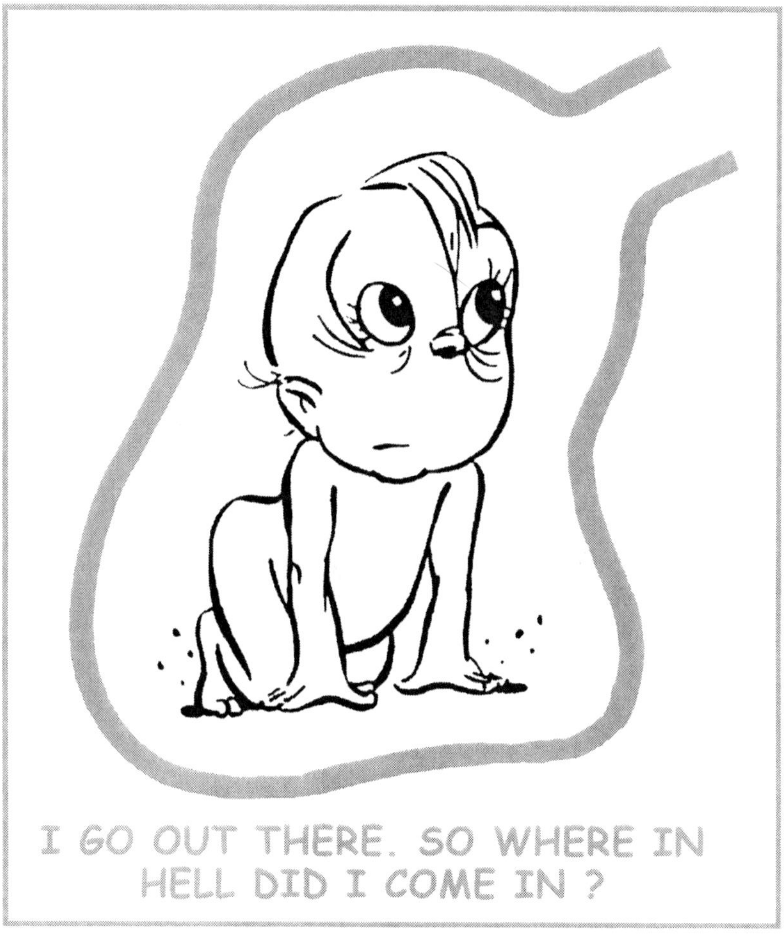
I GO OUT THERE. SO WHERE IN
HELL DID I COME IN ?

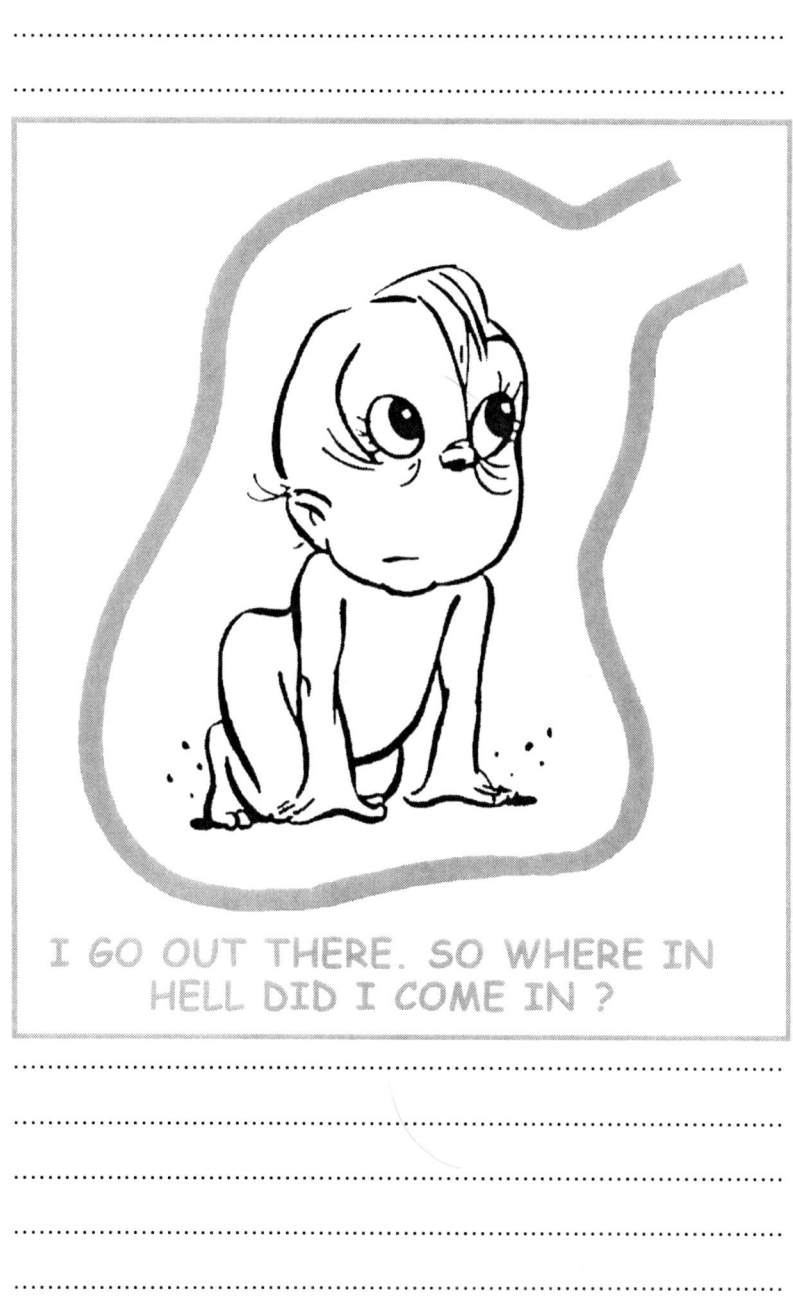

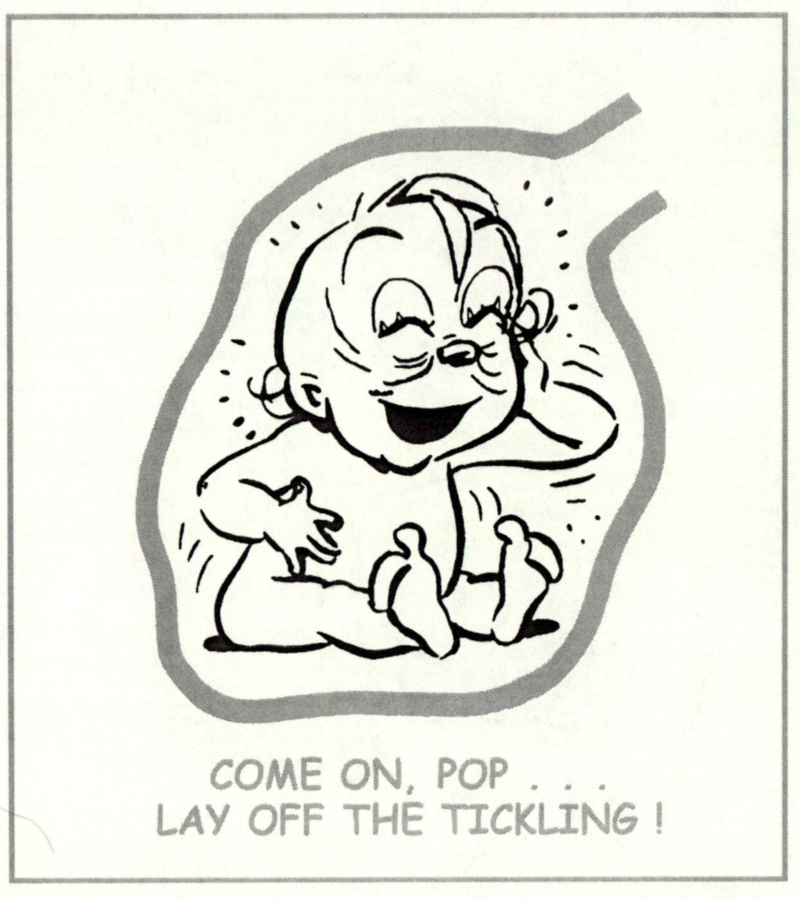

COME ON, POP . . .
LAY OFF THE TICKLING !

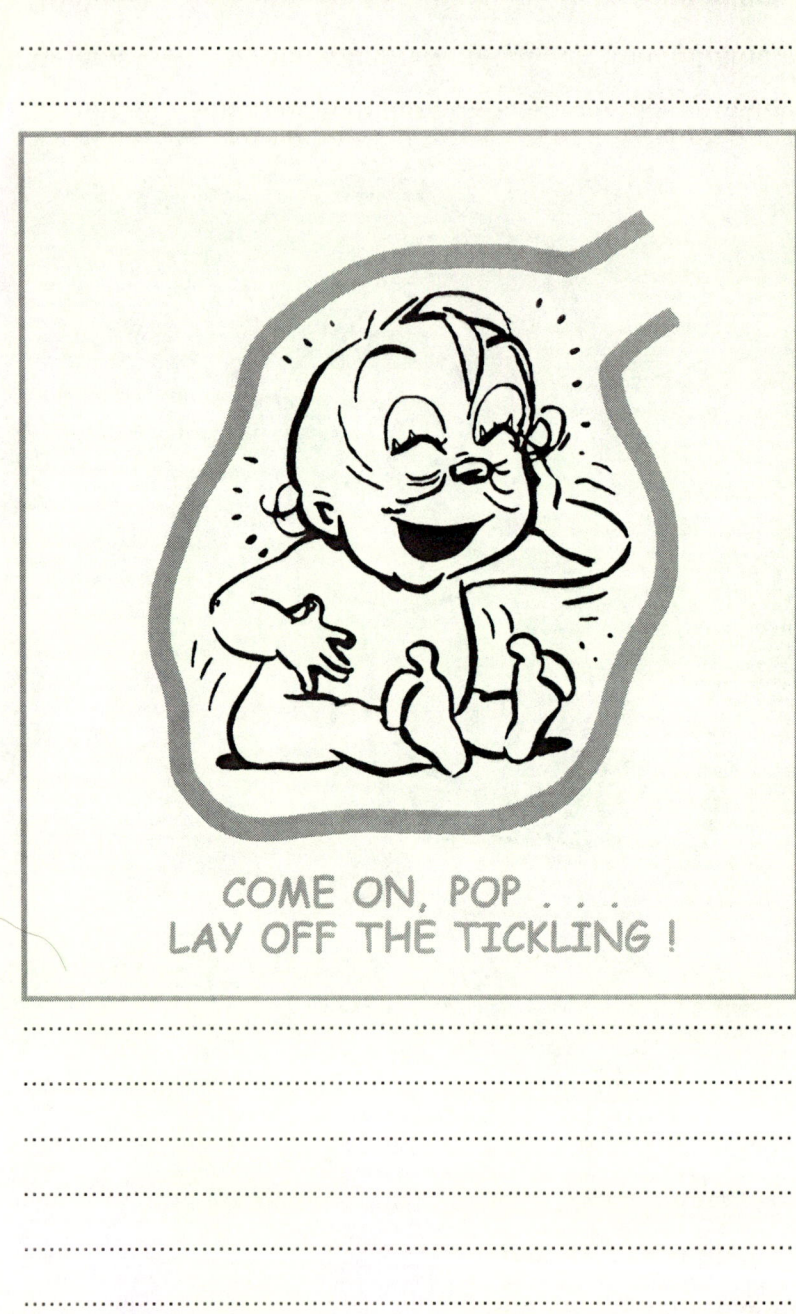

BOY! CAN WOMEN TALK DIRTY!

Your Grandparents:

....
....
....
....
....
....
....
....
....
....

Your Other Grandparents:

....
....
....
....
....
....
....
....
....
....
....
....
....

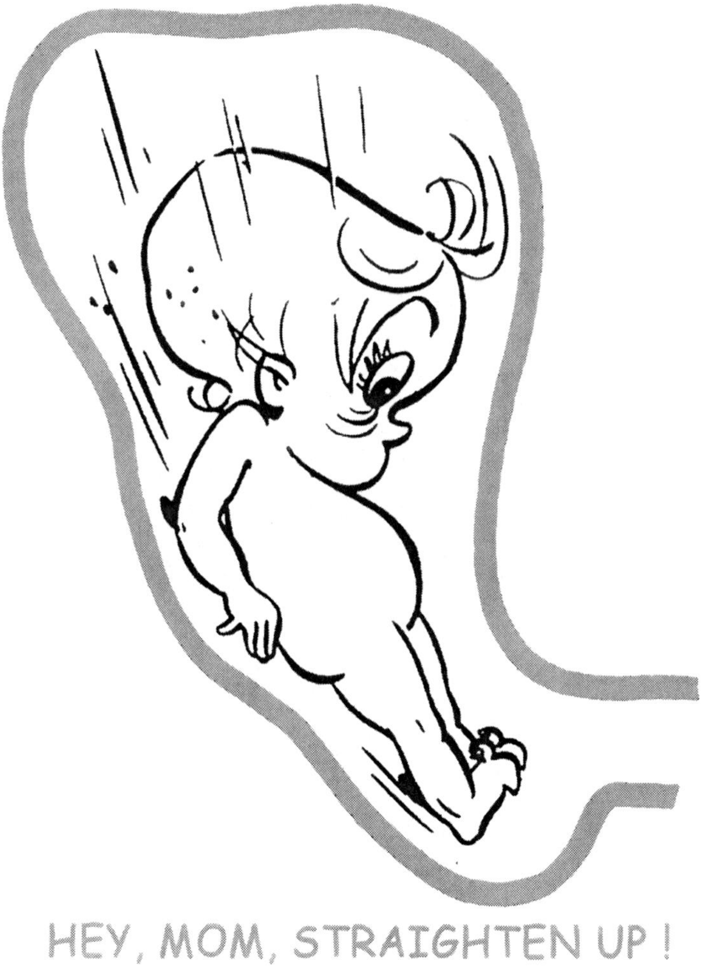

HEY, MOM, STRAIGHTEN UP !

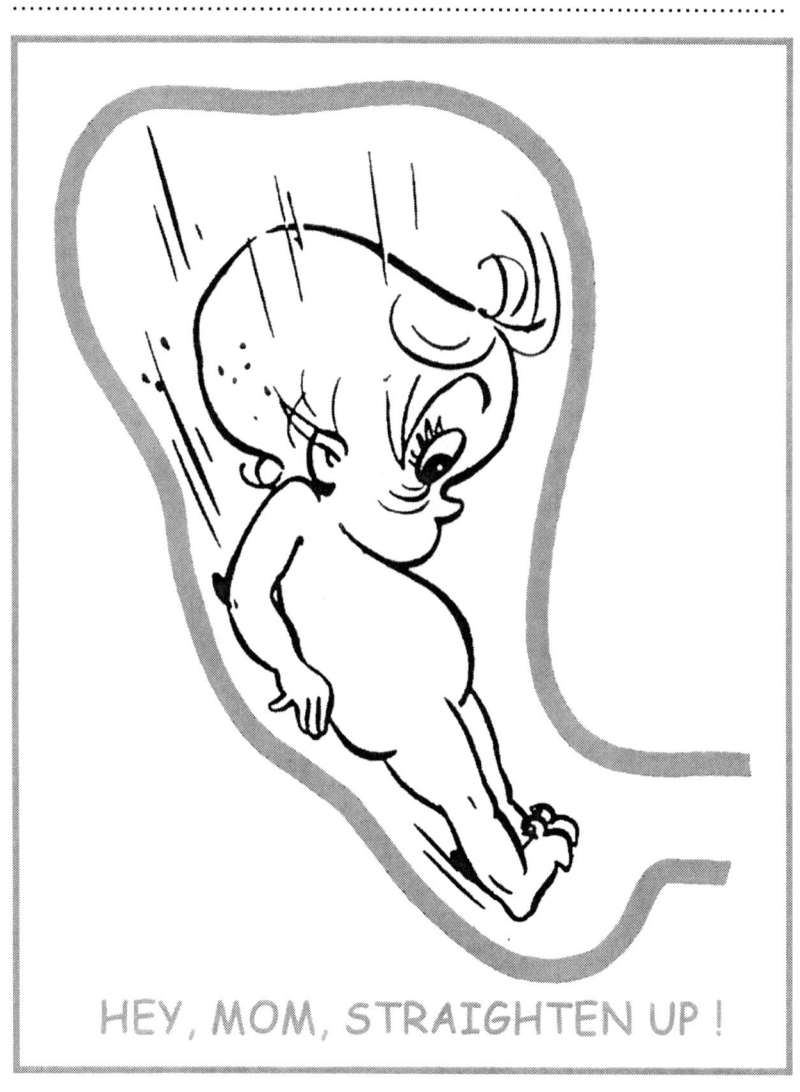

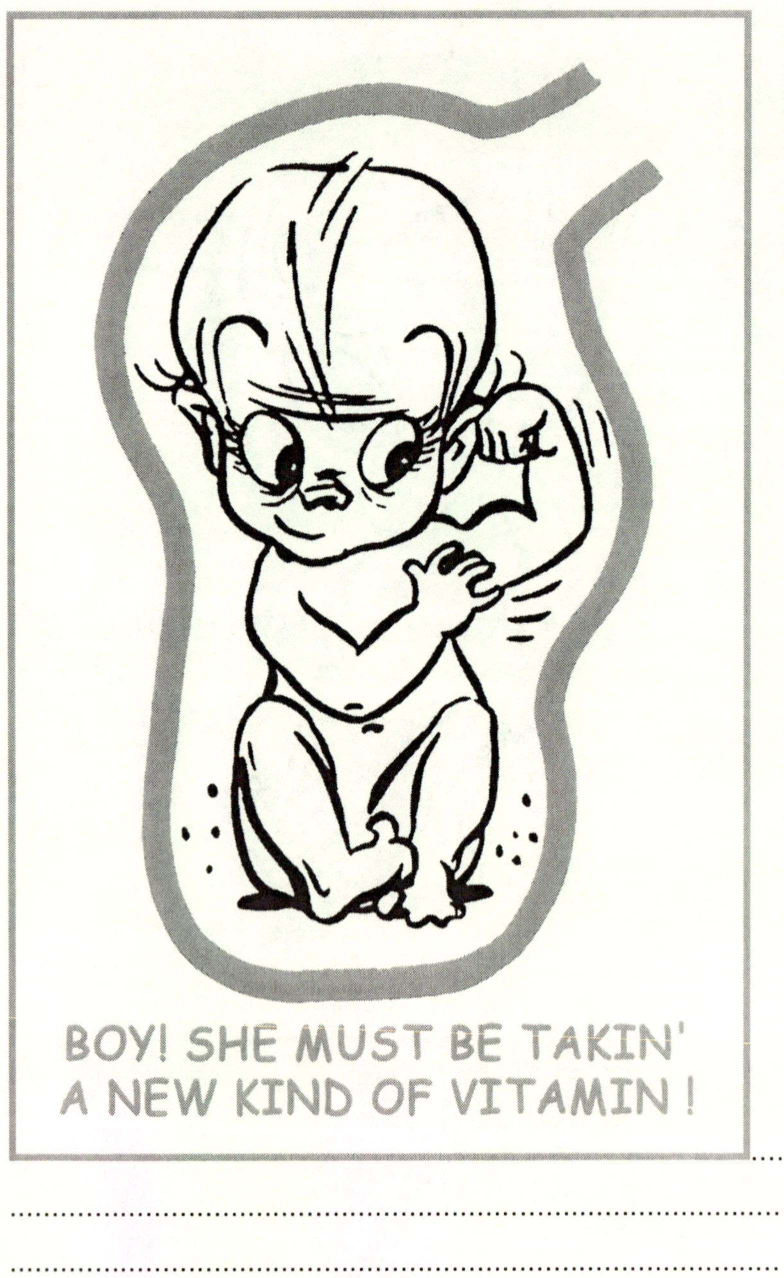

BOY! SHE MUST BE TAKIN'
A NEW KIND OF VITAMIN !

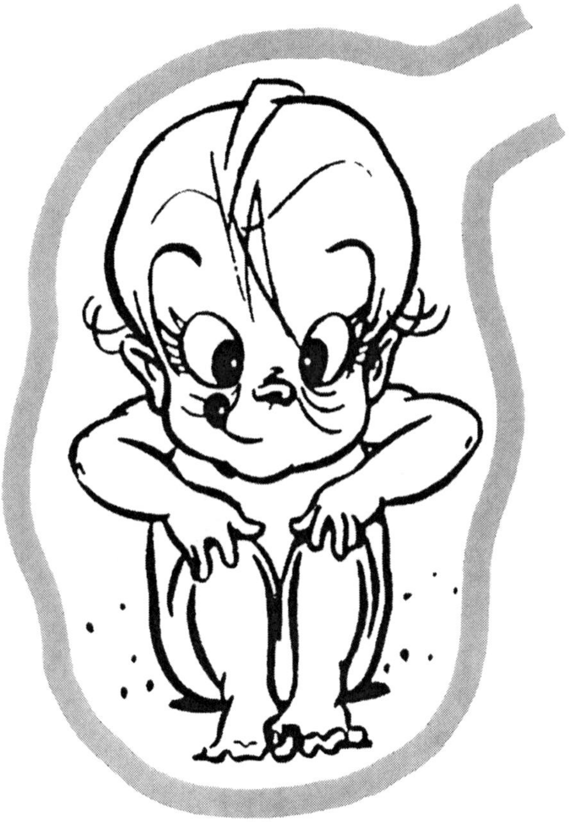

MAN, WHAT I WOULDN'T GIVE
FOR A HOT DOG
WITH PLENTY OF MUSTARD !

I Suspected I Was Pregnant When:

....
....
....
....
....
....
....

How It Was Confirmed:

....
....
....
....
....
....
....
....
....
....

Our Doctor:

....
....
....
....
....

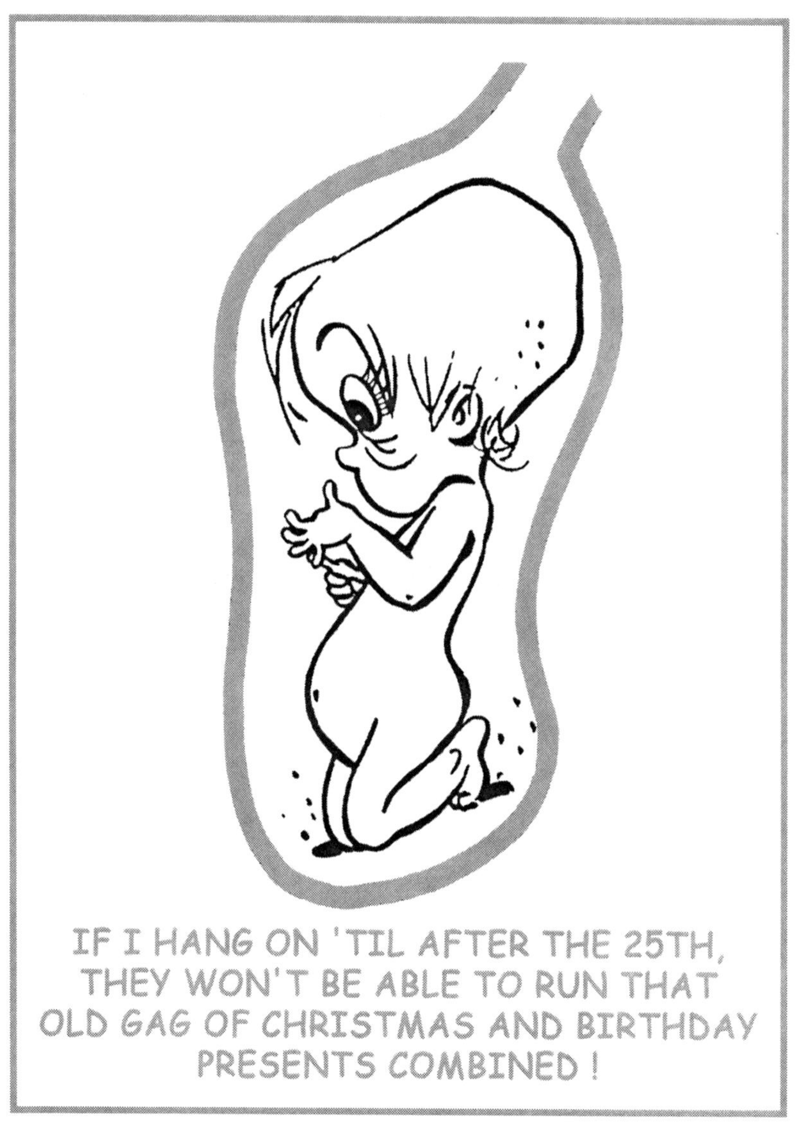

IF I HANG ON 'TIL AFTER THE 25TH, THEY WON'T BE ABLE TO RUN THAT OLD GAG OF CHRISTMAS AND BIRTHDAY PRESENTS COMBINED !

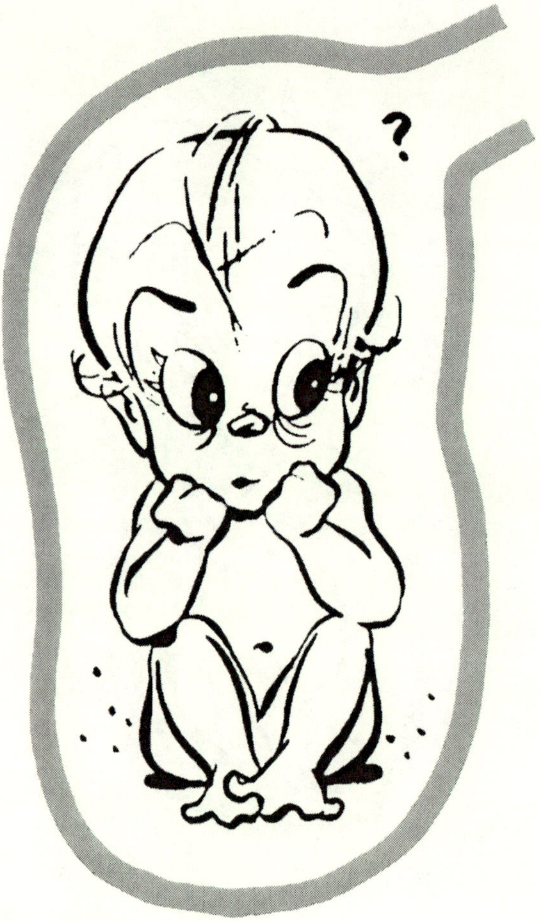

SHE'S PICKING A HELLUVA TIME
TO GO HOME TO MOTHER!

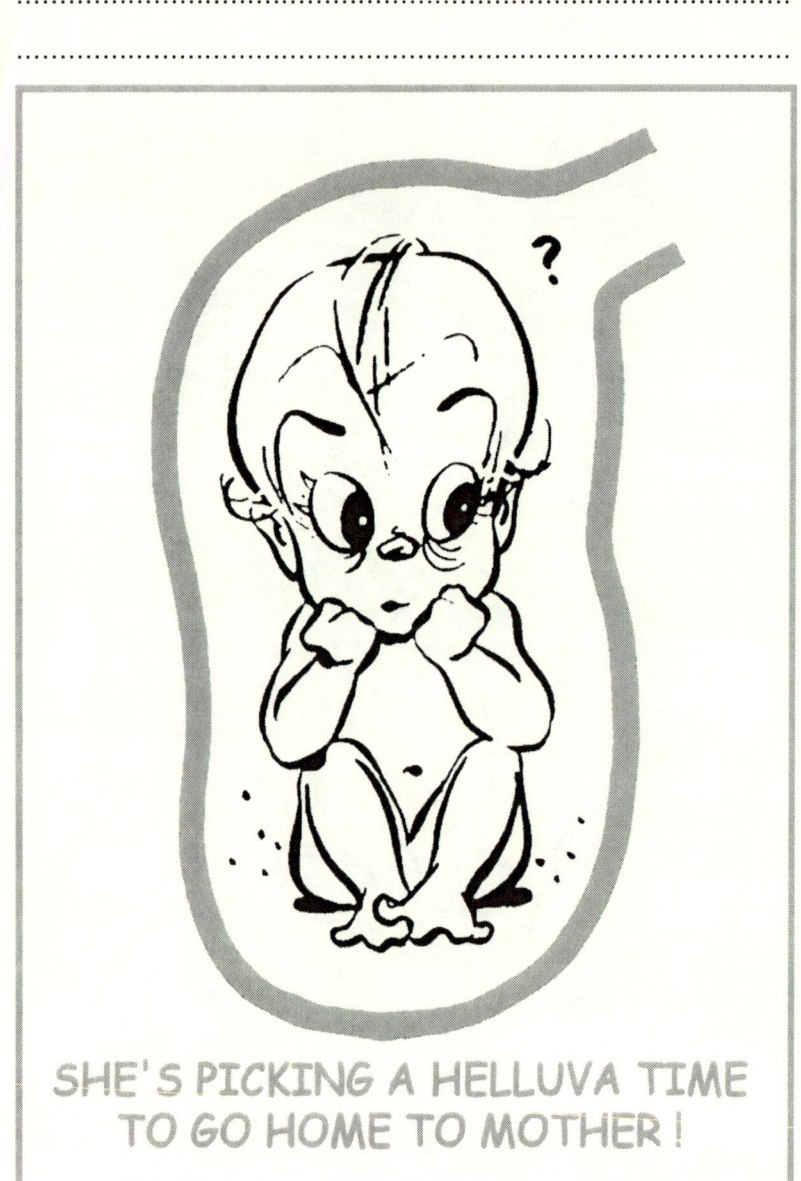

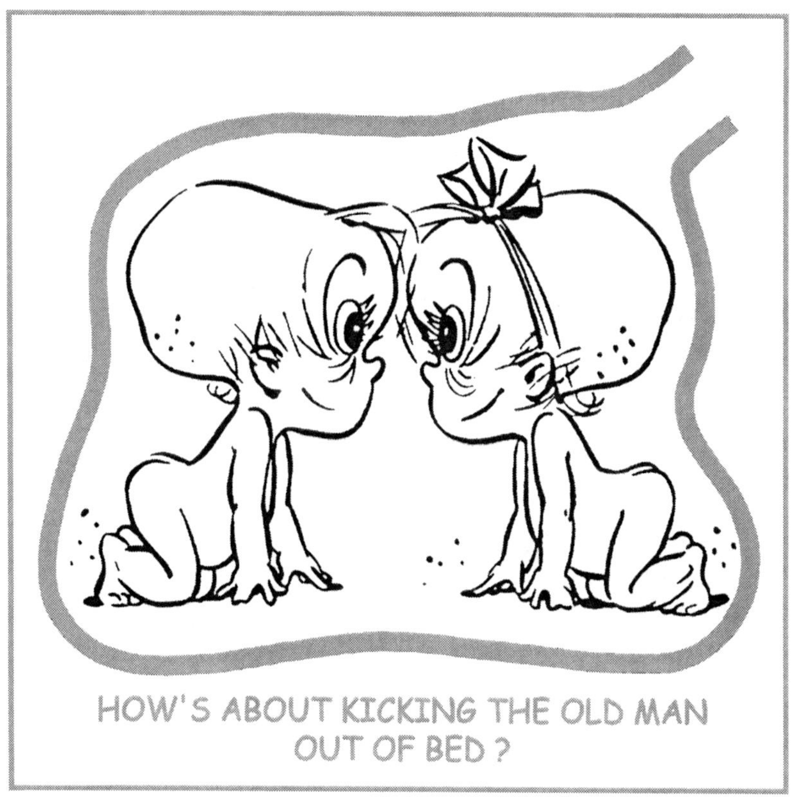

HOW'S ABOUT KICKING THE OLD MAN OUT OF BED ?

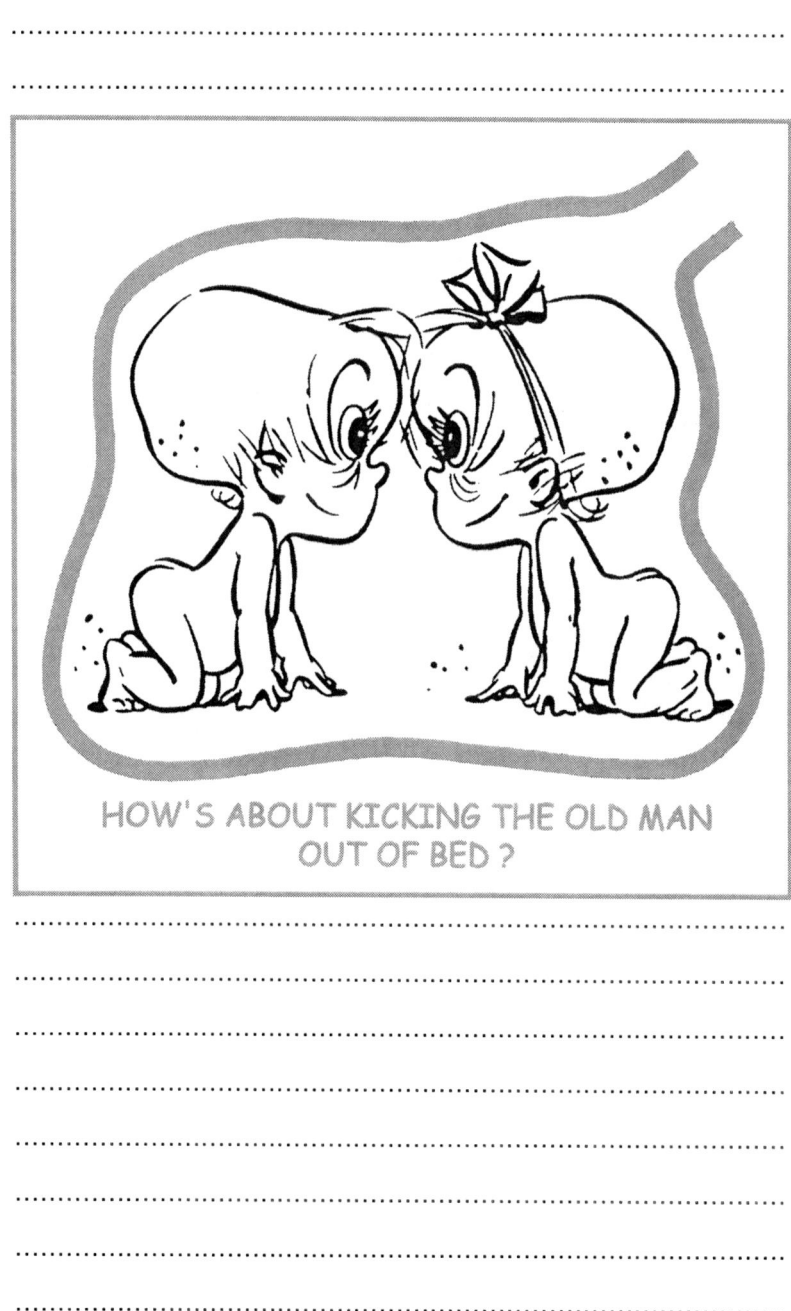

How We Felt About It:

....
....
....
....
....
....
....

Why I Was Thrilled:

....
....
....
....
....
....
....

Why I Was Nervous:

....
....
....
....
....
....
....
....
....

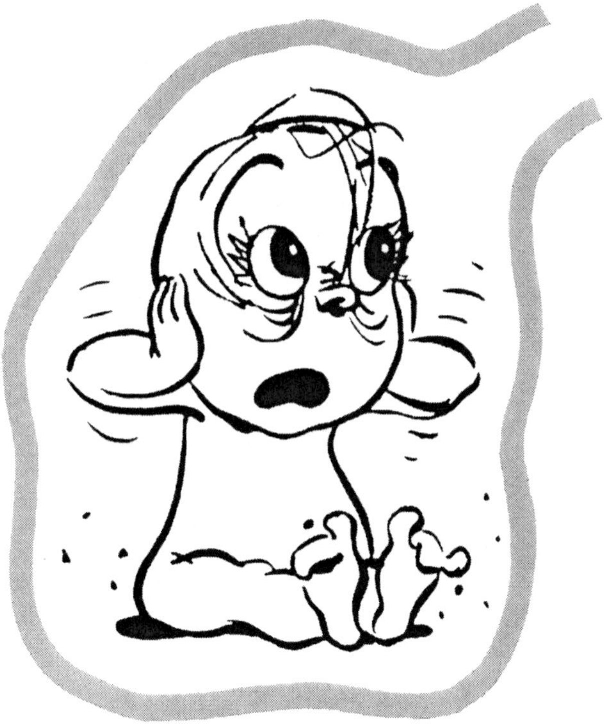

FOR THE LOVA PETE, SWALLOW THAT DAMN PEANUT BRITTLE !

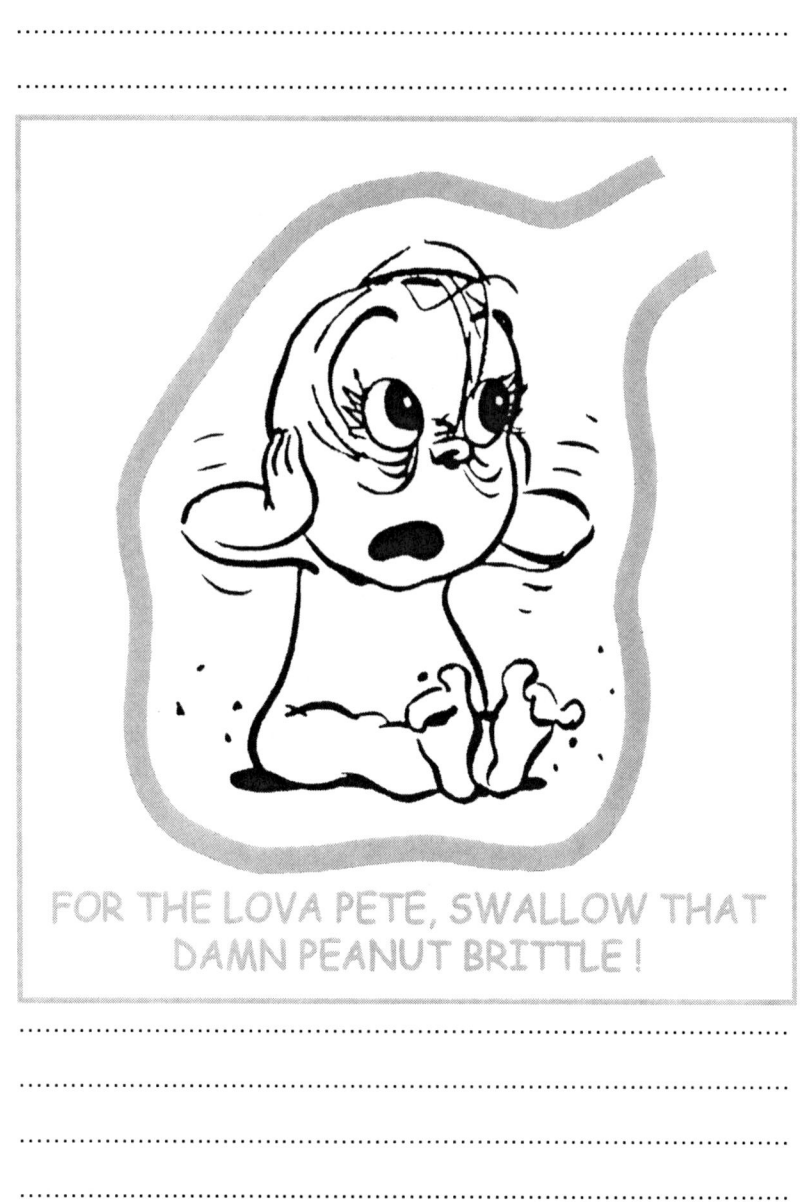

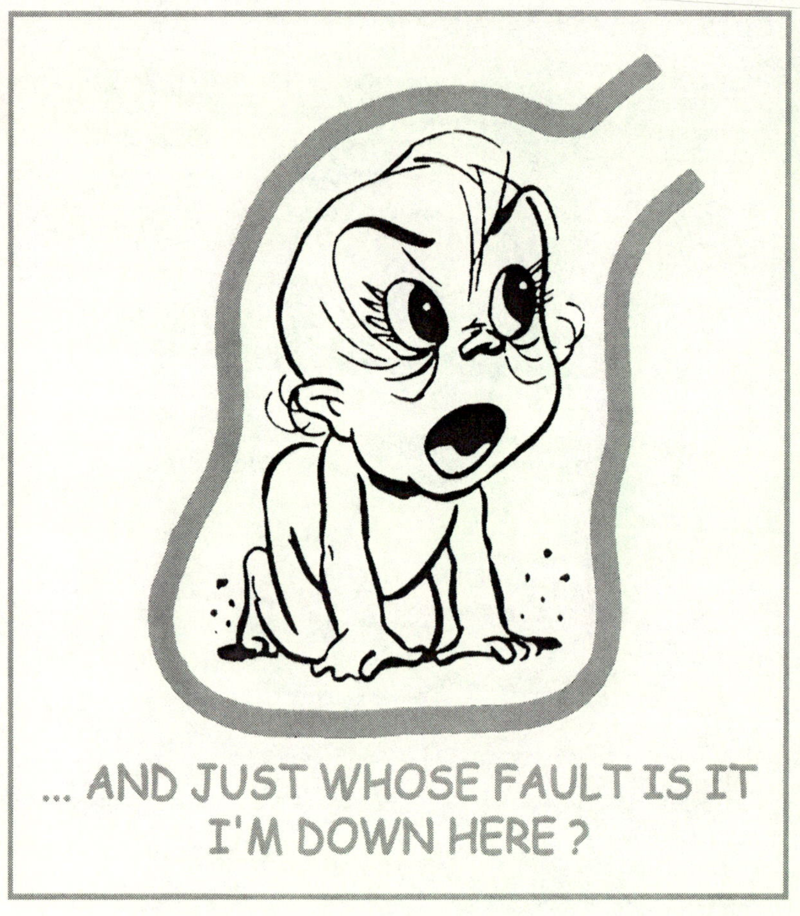

... AND JUST WHOSE FAULT IS IT I'M DOWN HERE ?

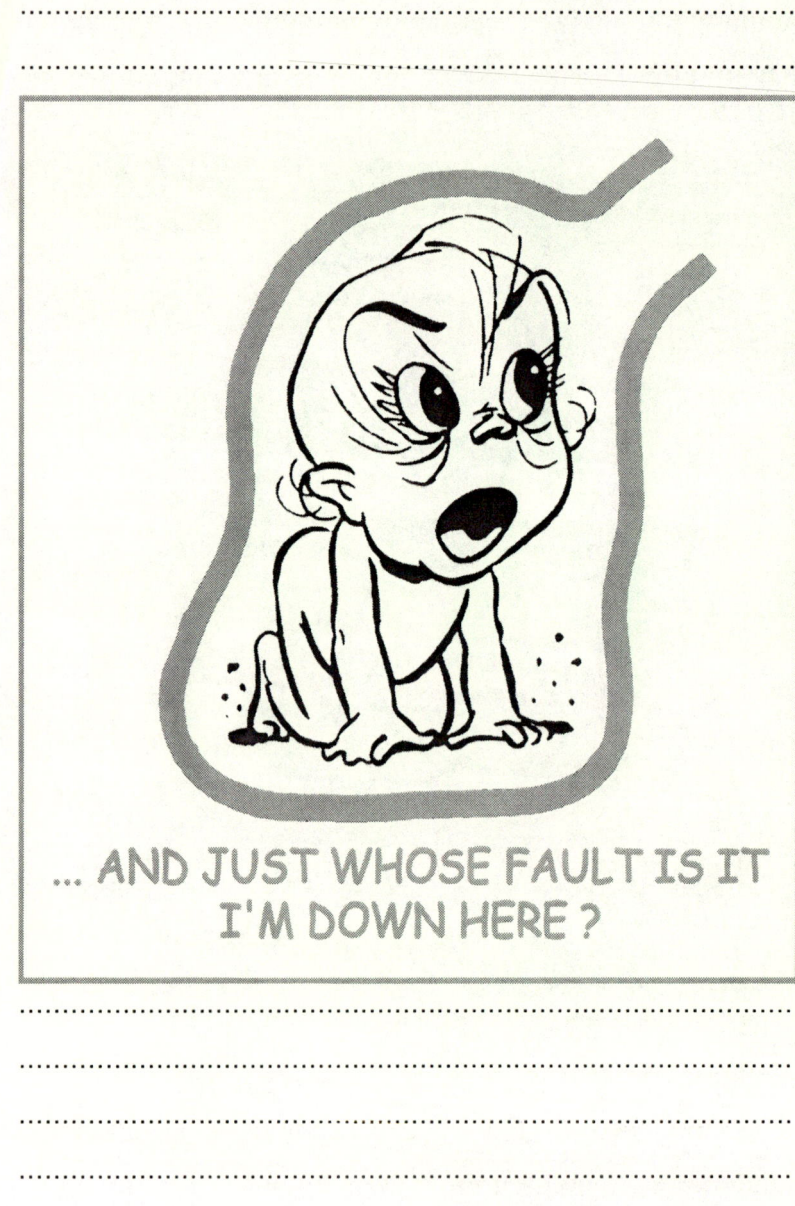

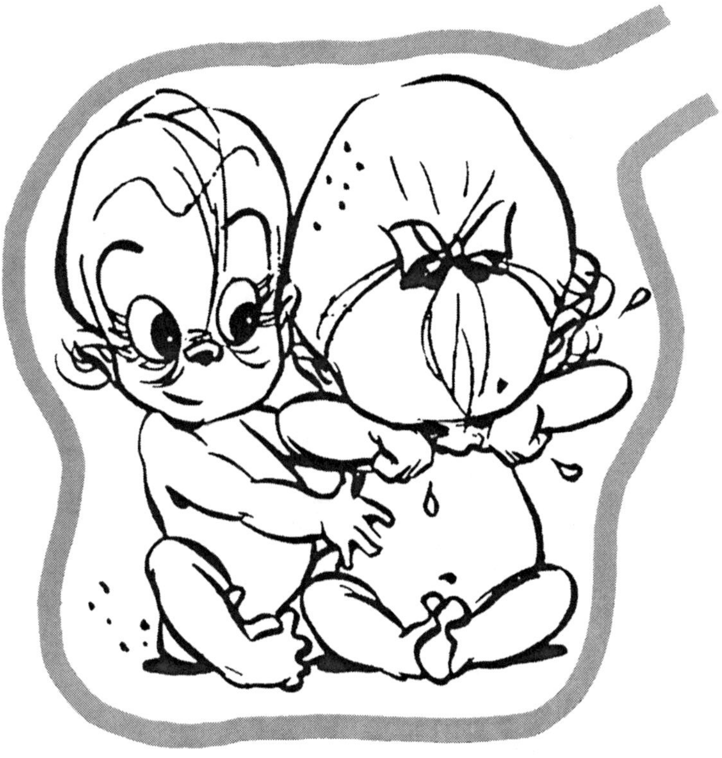

YOU ARE TOO, FULLY EQUIPPED !

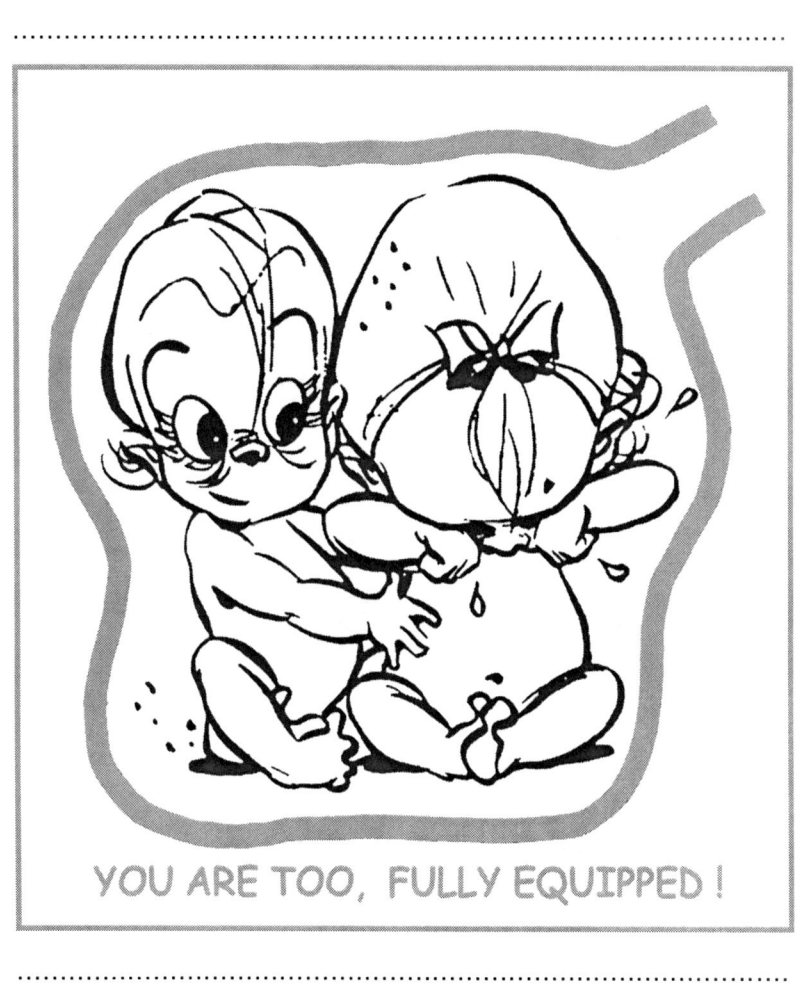

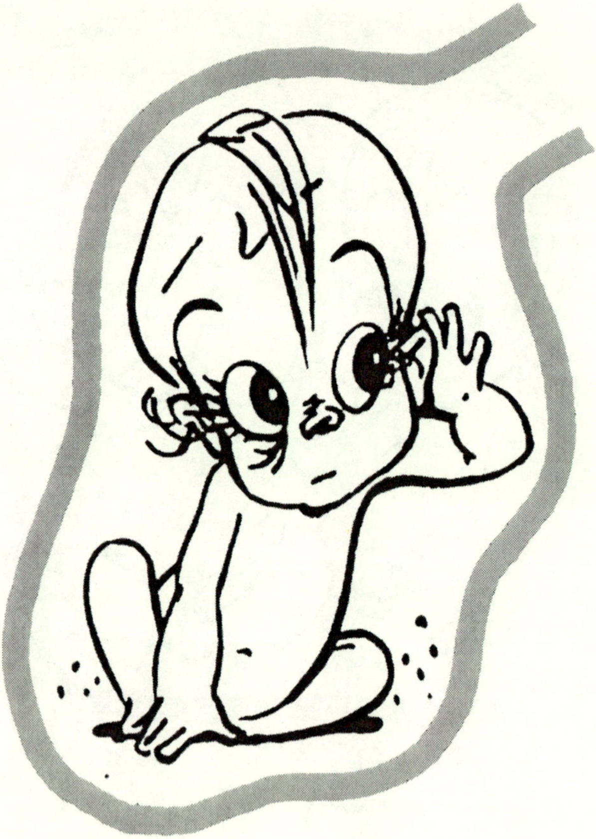

THAT DOC MUST THINK HE'S TAPPING A WATERMELON!

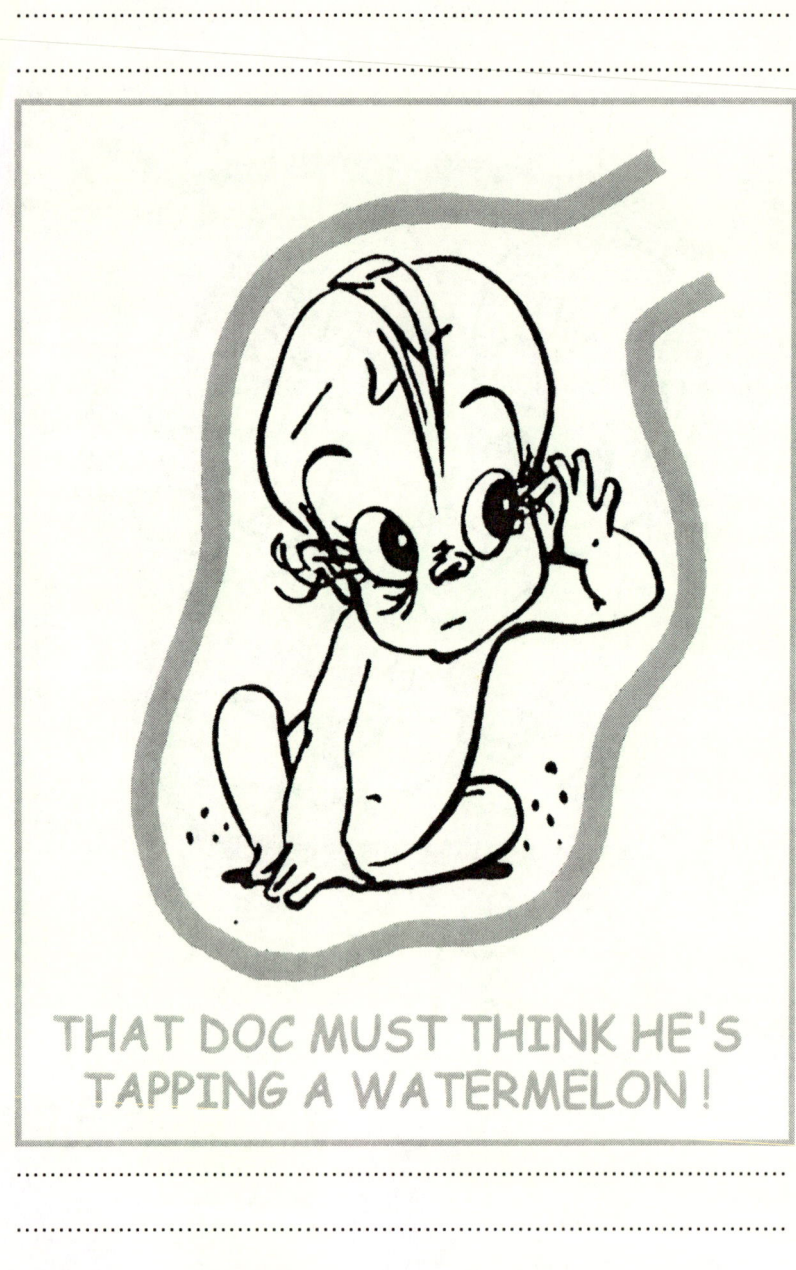

NOTHING'S LOOSE. SHE'S SHOOTING CRAPS WITH THE MILKMAN!

What your Grandparents Said:

....
....
....
....
....
....
....
....
....
....
....

And Your OTHER Grandparents Said:

....
....
....
....
....
....
....
....
....
....
....
....
....
....

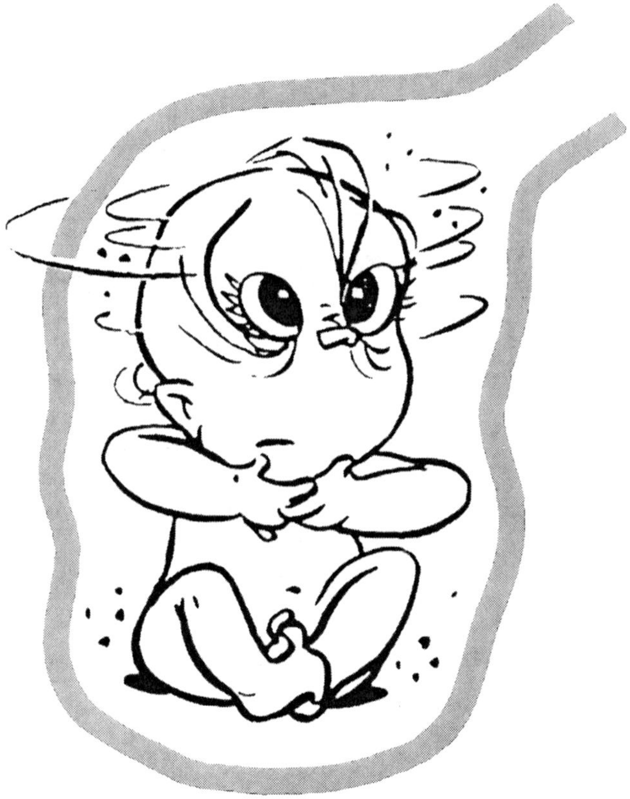

OH BROTHER! SHE'S SWIMMING UNDERWATER AGAIN!

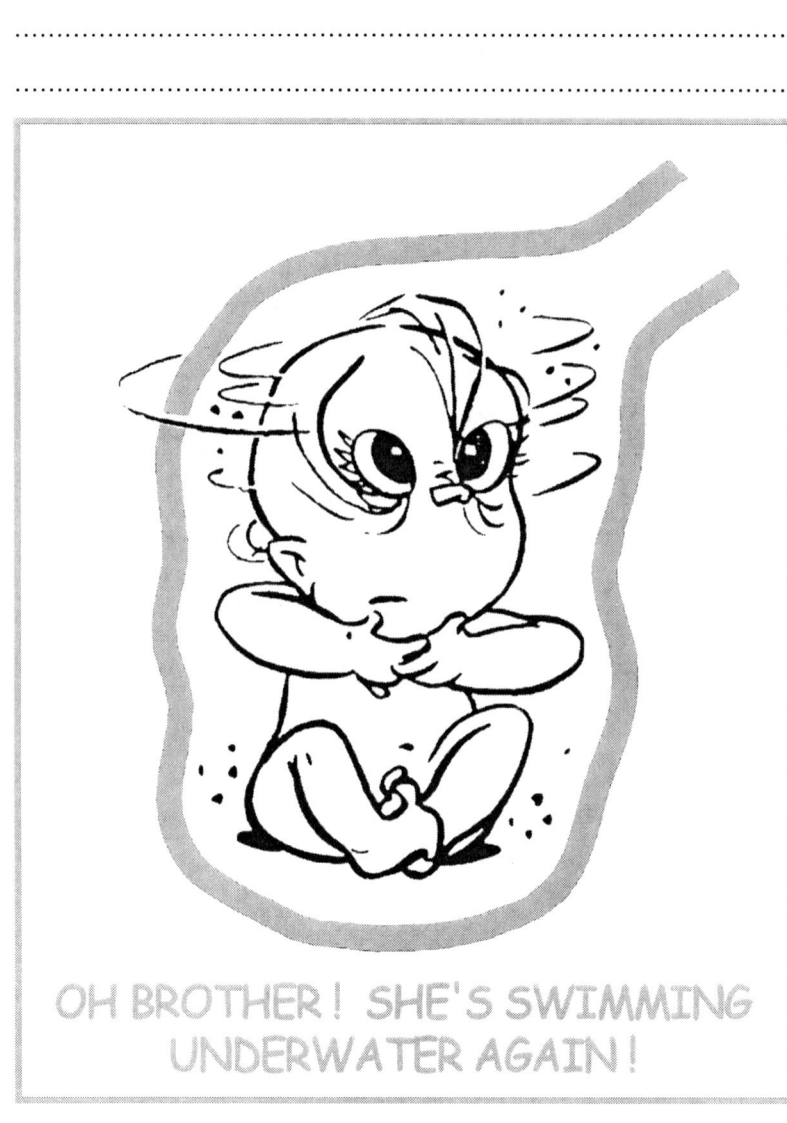

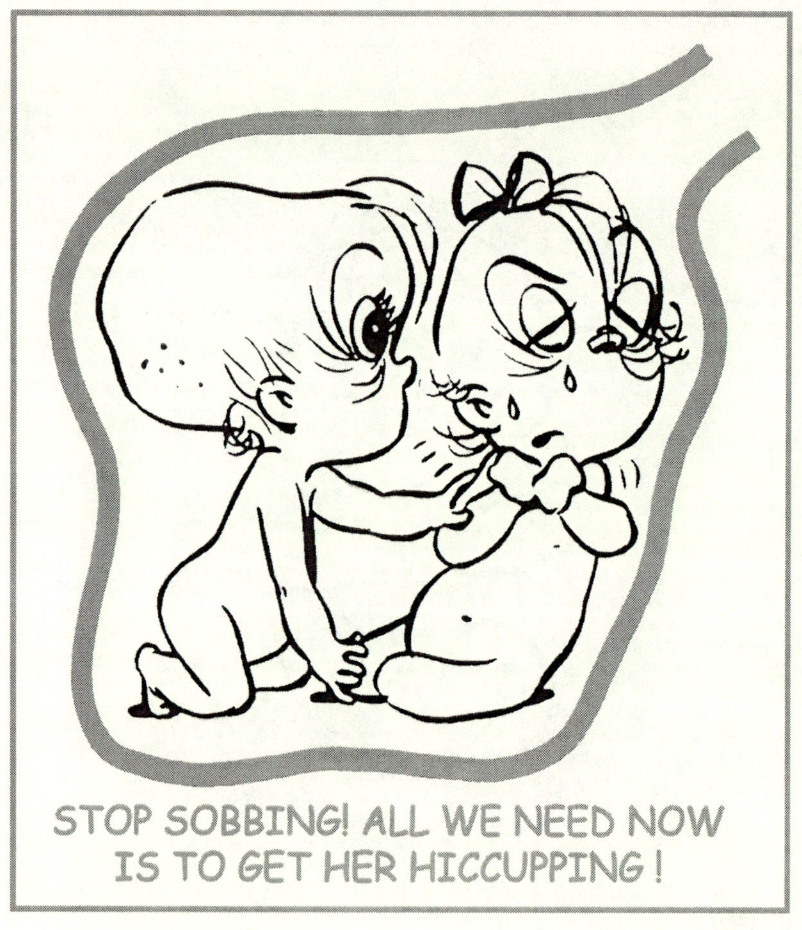

STOP SOBBING! ALL WE NEED NOW IS TO GET HER HICCUPPING !

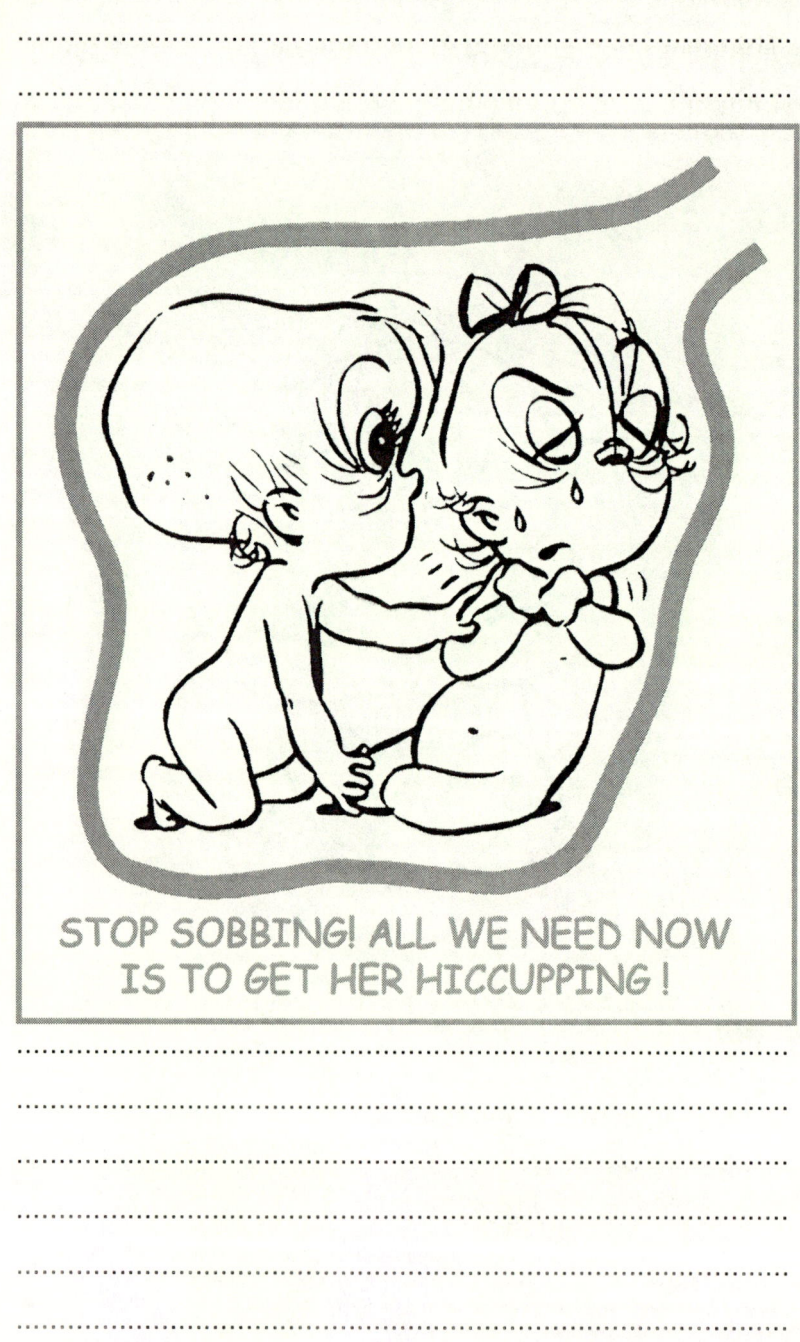

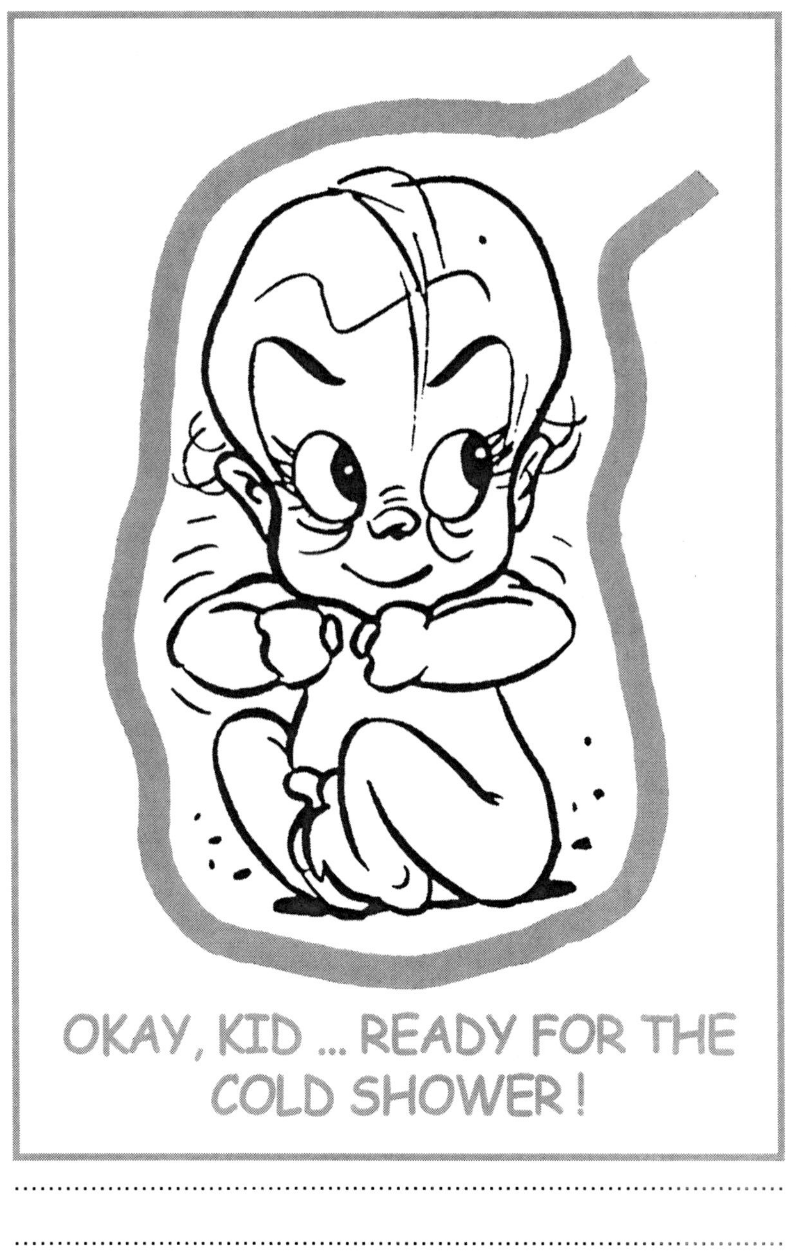

OKAY, KID ... READY FOR THE COLD SHOWER!

How We Celebrated:

....
....
....
....
....
....
....
....
....
....
....
....
....
....

Who's Most Excited:

....
....
....
....
....
....
....
....
....
....
....

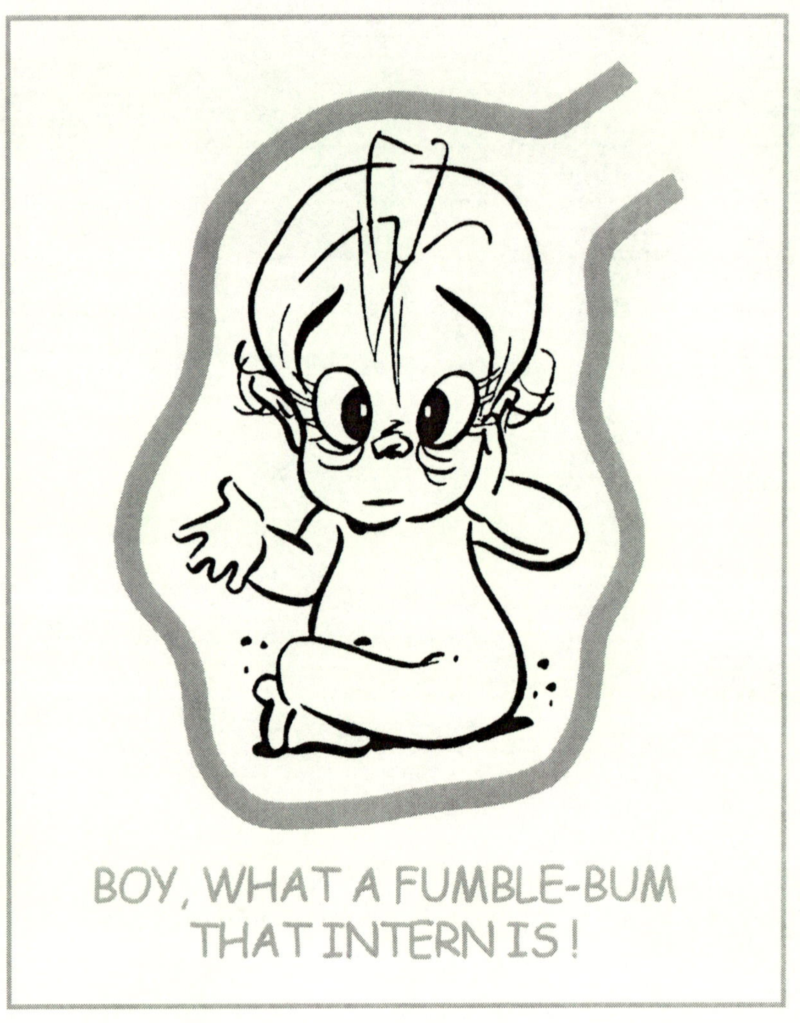

BOY, WHAT A FUMBLE-BUM
THAT INTERN IS!

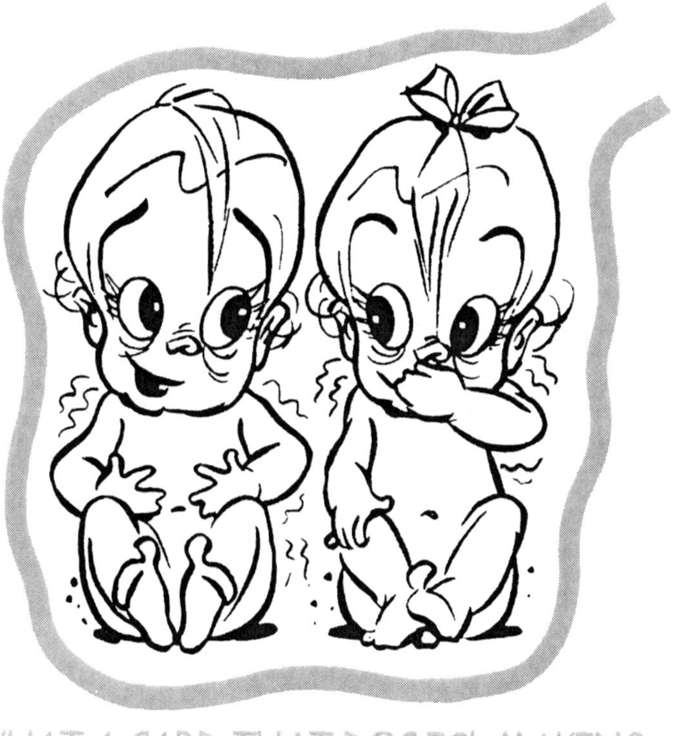

WHAT A CARD THAT DOC IS! MAKING HER DIET TO KEEP ME SMALL !

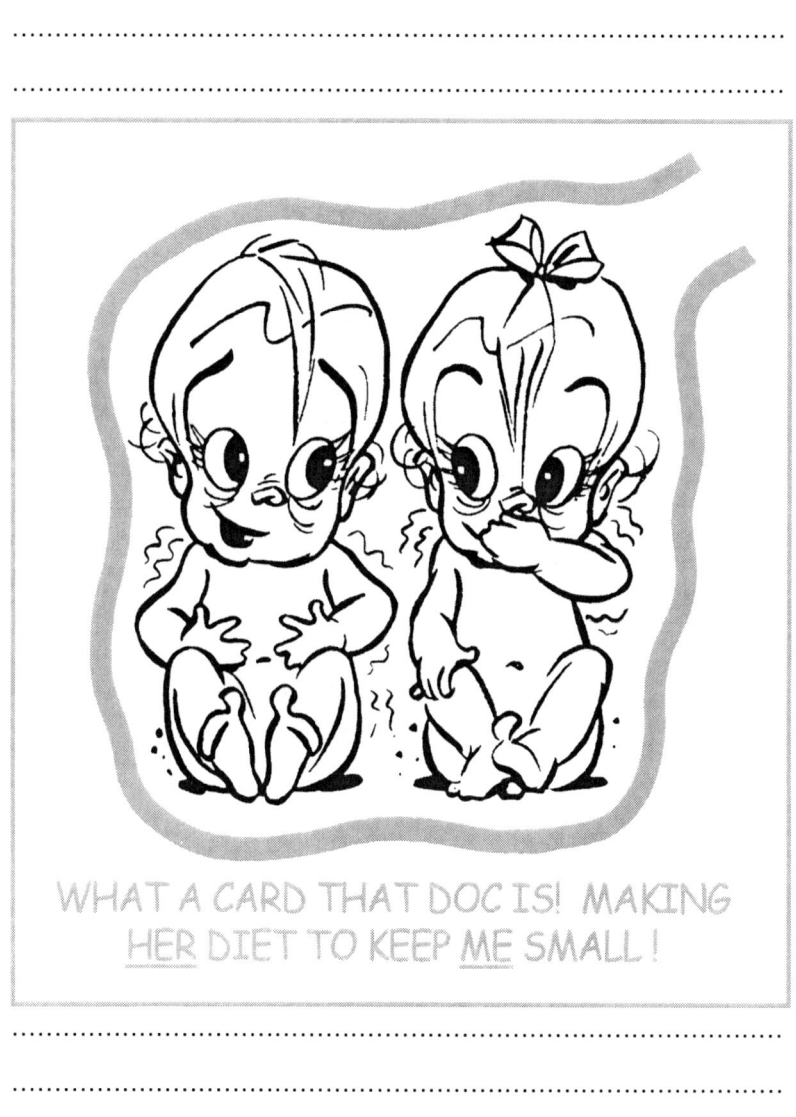

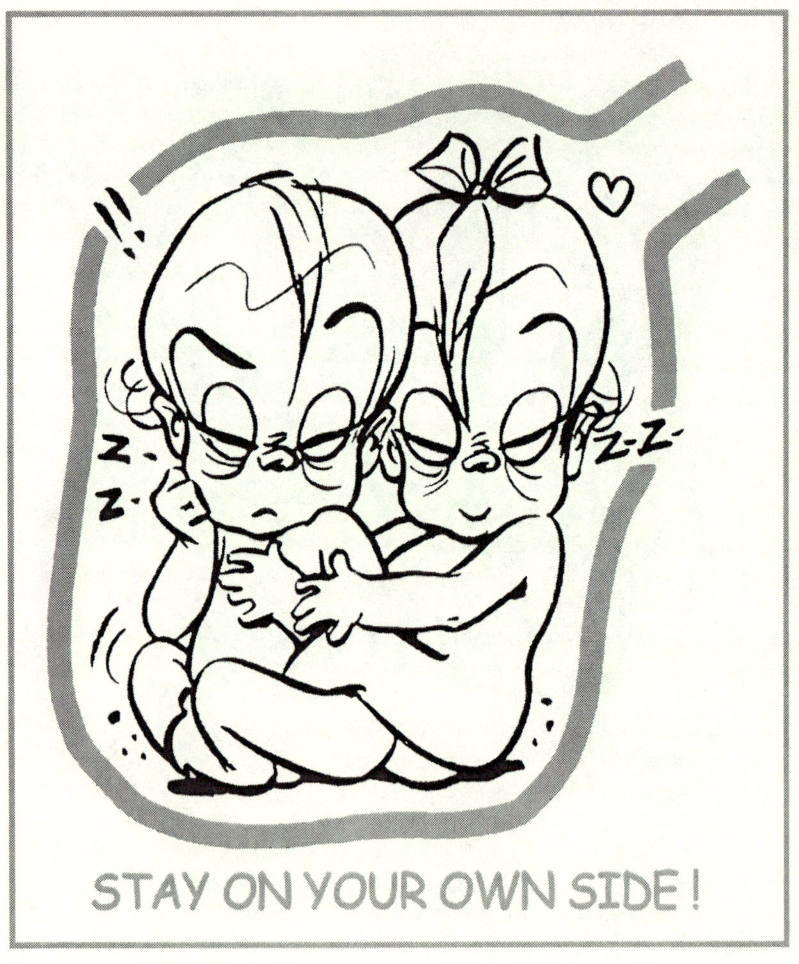

Z-Z-

STAY ON YOUR OWN SIDE !

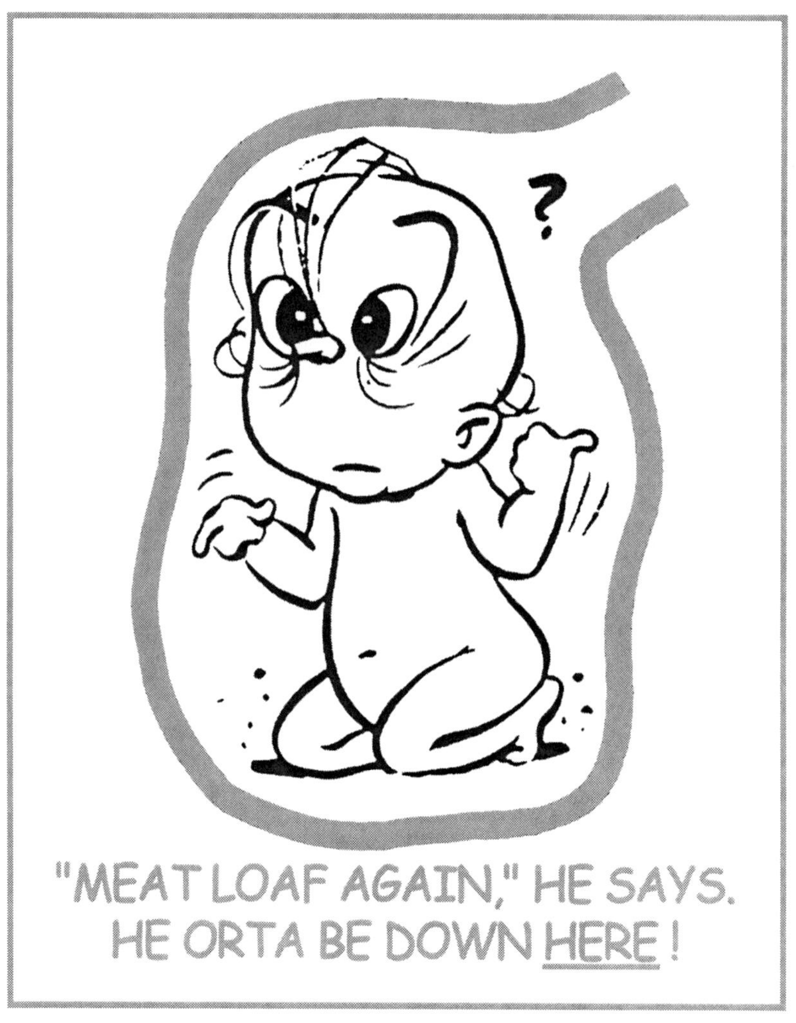
?

"MEAT LOAF AGAIN," HE SAYS.
HE ORTA BE DOWN HERE !

Your First Baby Gift:

....
....
....
....
....
....

From Who:

....
....
....
....

How I Felt About Being Pregnant:

....
....
....
....
....
....
....
....
....
....
....
....
....
....

HOW CAN YOU BE SEASICK?
SHE'S ONLY TAKING A BATH!

OKAY, ONE MORE DANCE AND THEN LET'S GET THE HELL HOME!

Our First Visit to the Doctor:

....
....
....
....
....
....
....
....
....

Stuff We Need to Remember:

....
....
....
....
....
....
....
....
....
....
....
....
....
....
....

MAN! IS SHE BITCHY TODAY!

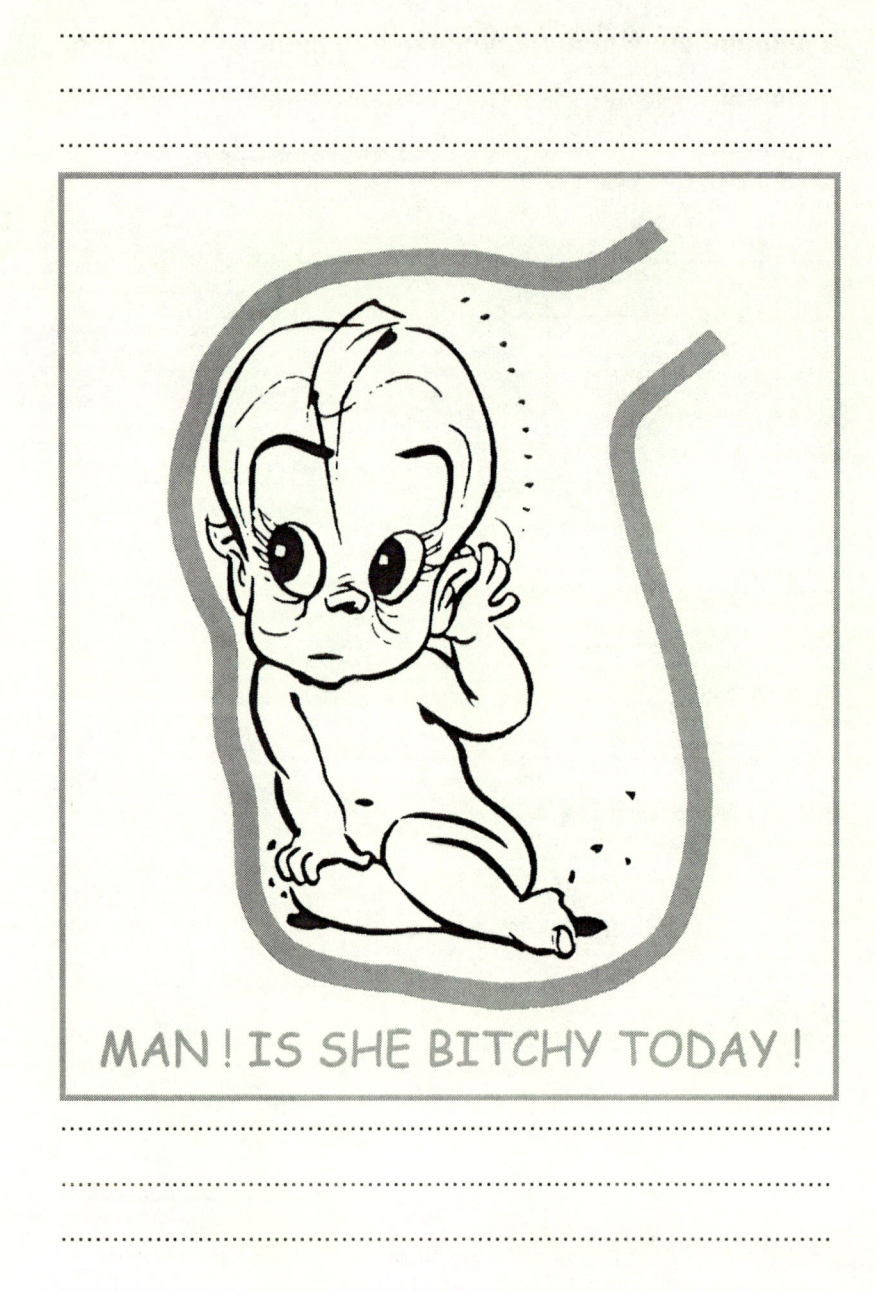

YOU MIGHT AS WELL LEARN THIS NOW AS LATER ... IT'E JUST AS EASY TO SNAG A RICH HUSBAND AS A POOR SCHNOOK!

IT'S GREAT THAT SHE'S PRACTICING WASHING THAT DOLL ... BUT THIS IS THE THIRD TIME SHE'S DROPPED IT!

OUCH! GET INTO THAT
HOT TUB A LITTLE SLOWER!

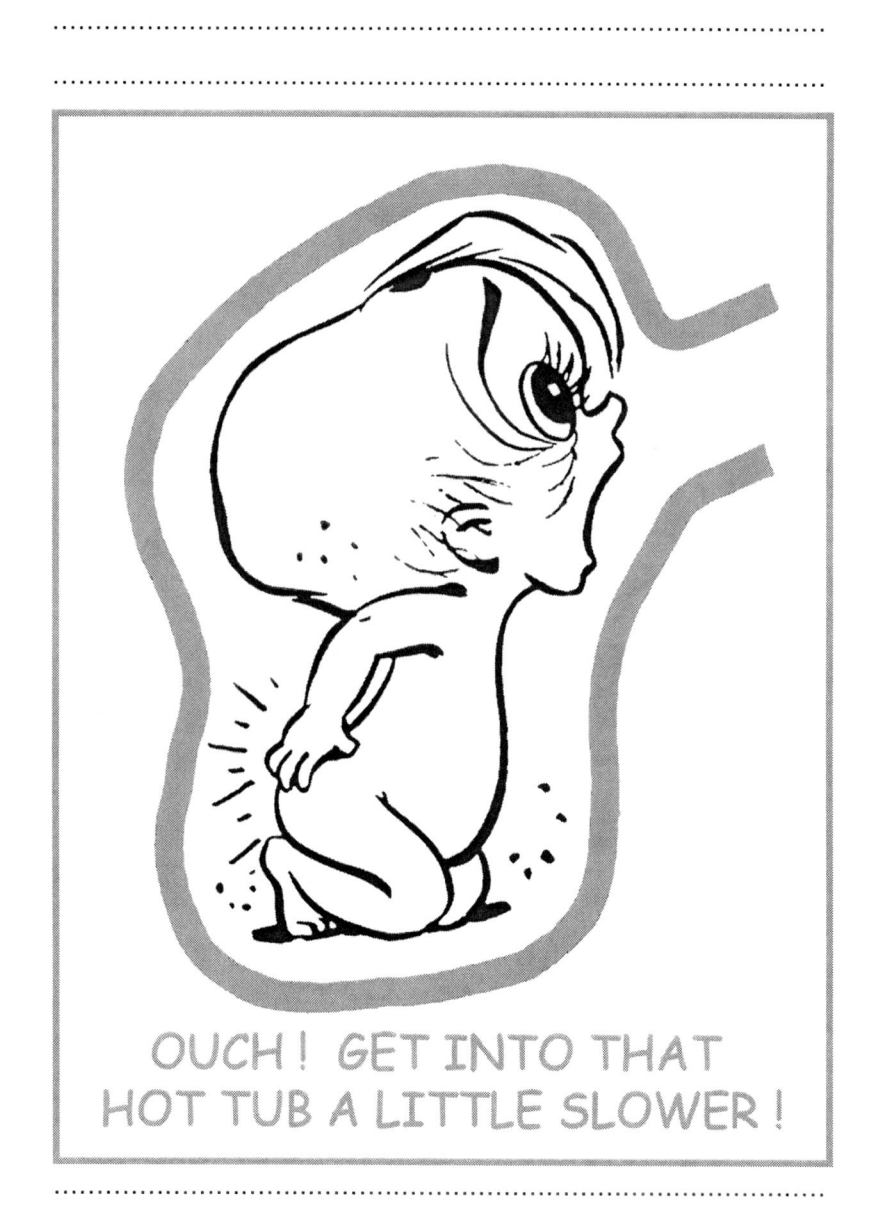

SURE IS COMFY WHEN SHE'S GOT HER LEGS UP!

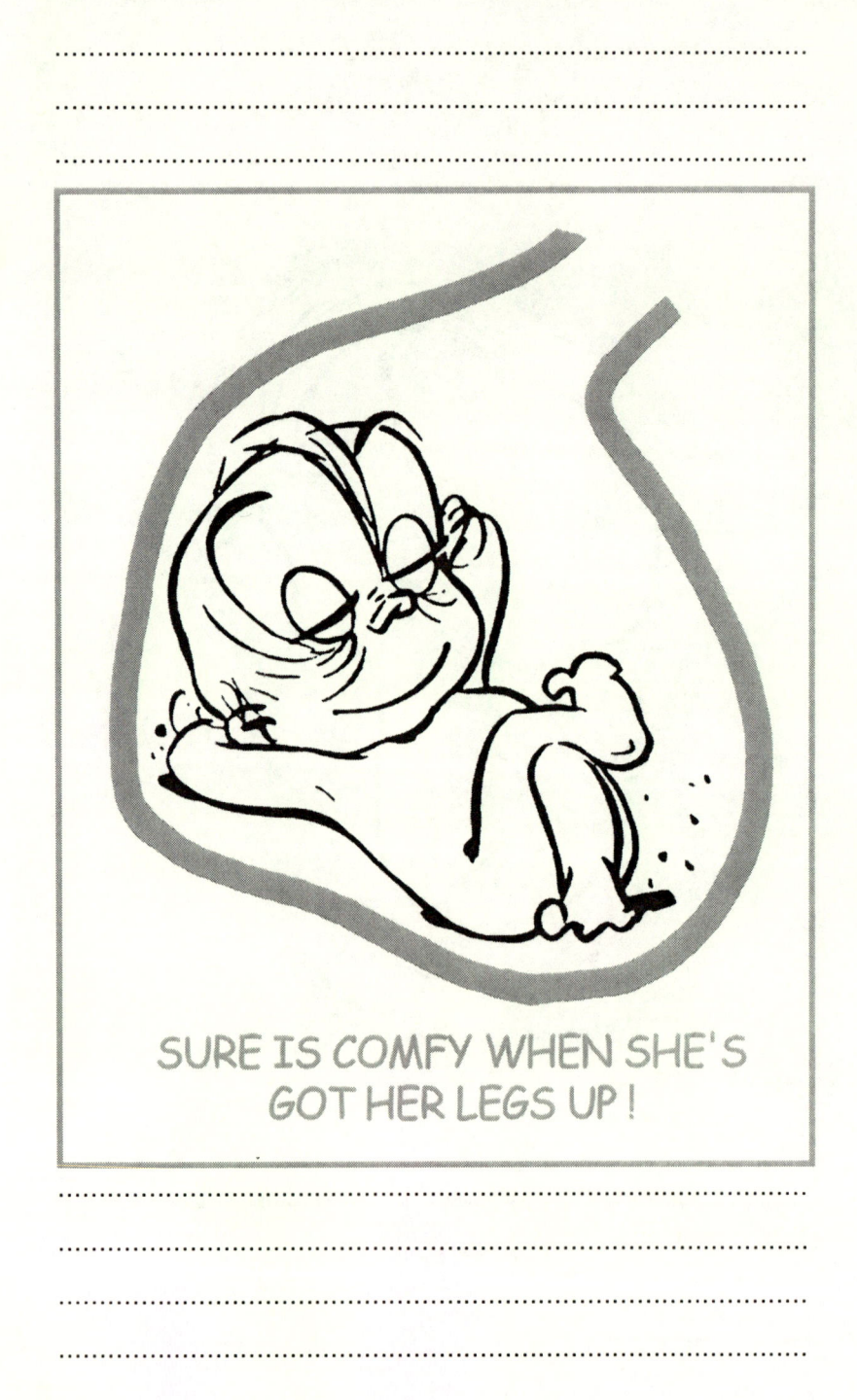

HOW CAN YOU CHEW A STEAK WITH NO TEETH?

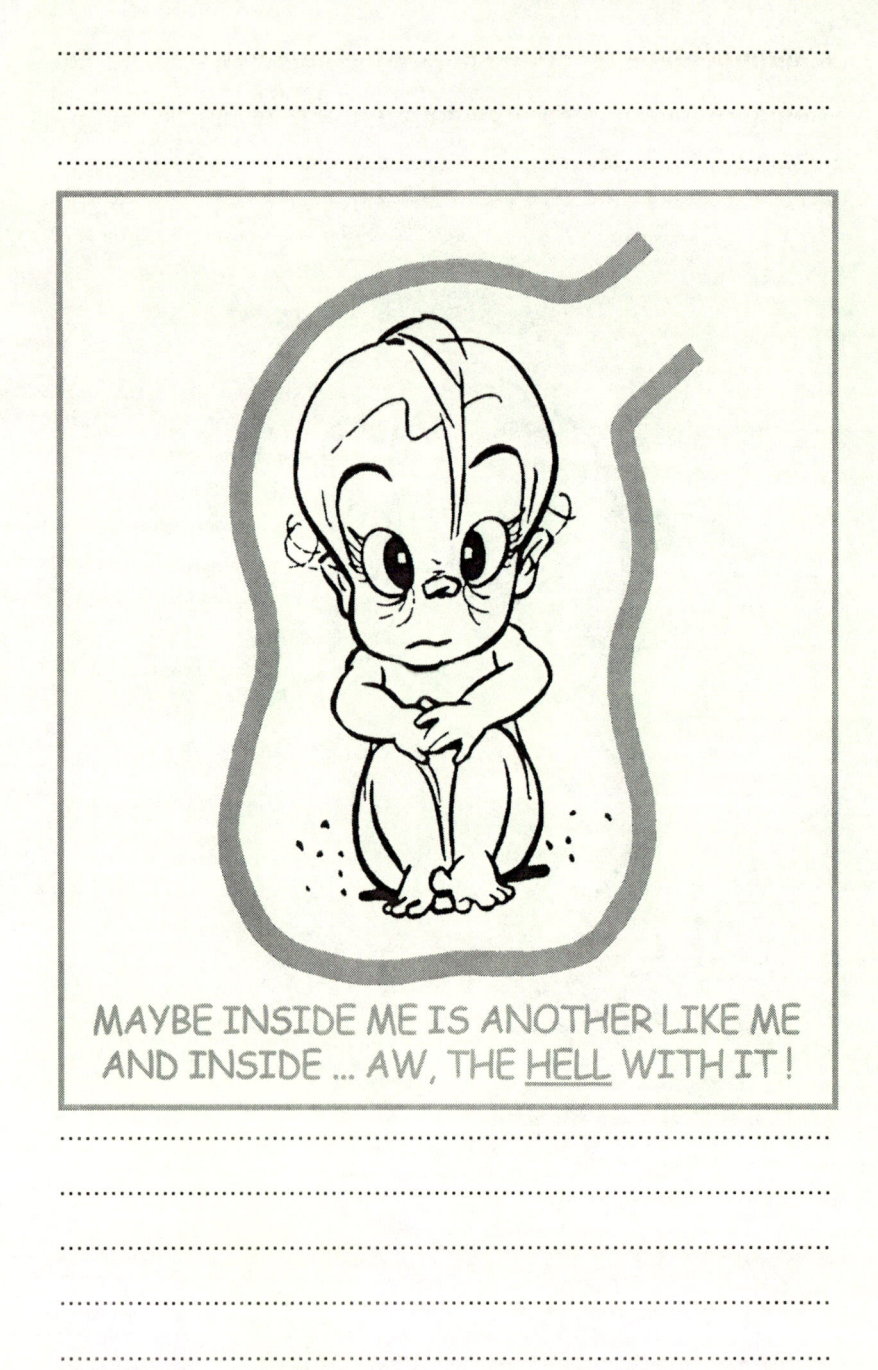

MAYBE INSIDE ME IS ANOTHER LIKE ME AND INSIDE ... AW, THE HELL WITH IT!

...I SAID, GET THAT GAW-DAMNED PURRIN' KITTY OFF YOUR LAP!

Strange Foods I Craved:
....
....
....
....
....
....
....
....
....
....

Foods I Can't Have:
....
....
....
....
....
....
....
....
....
....
....
....
....

YOUR PULSE IS NORMAL ... AND I'LL BE DAMN GLAD WHEN MOM TAKES YOU OVER!

EWWWW! SHE'S SUCKING LEMONS AGAIN!

Funny Memories So Far:

BOY! THE RUCKUS I COULD RAISE
WITH A FEATHER!

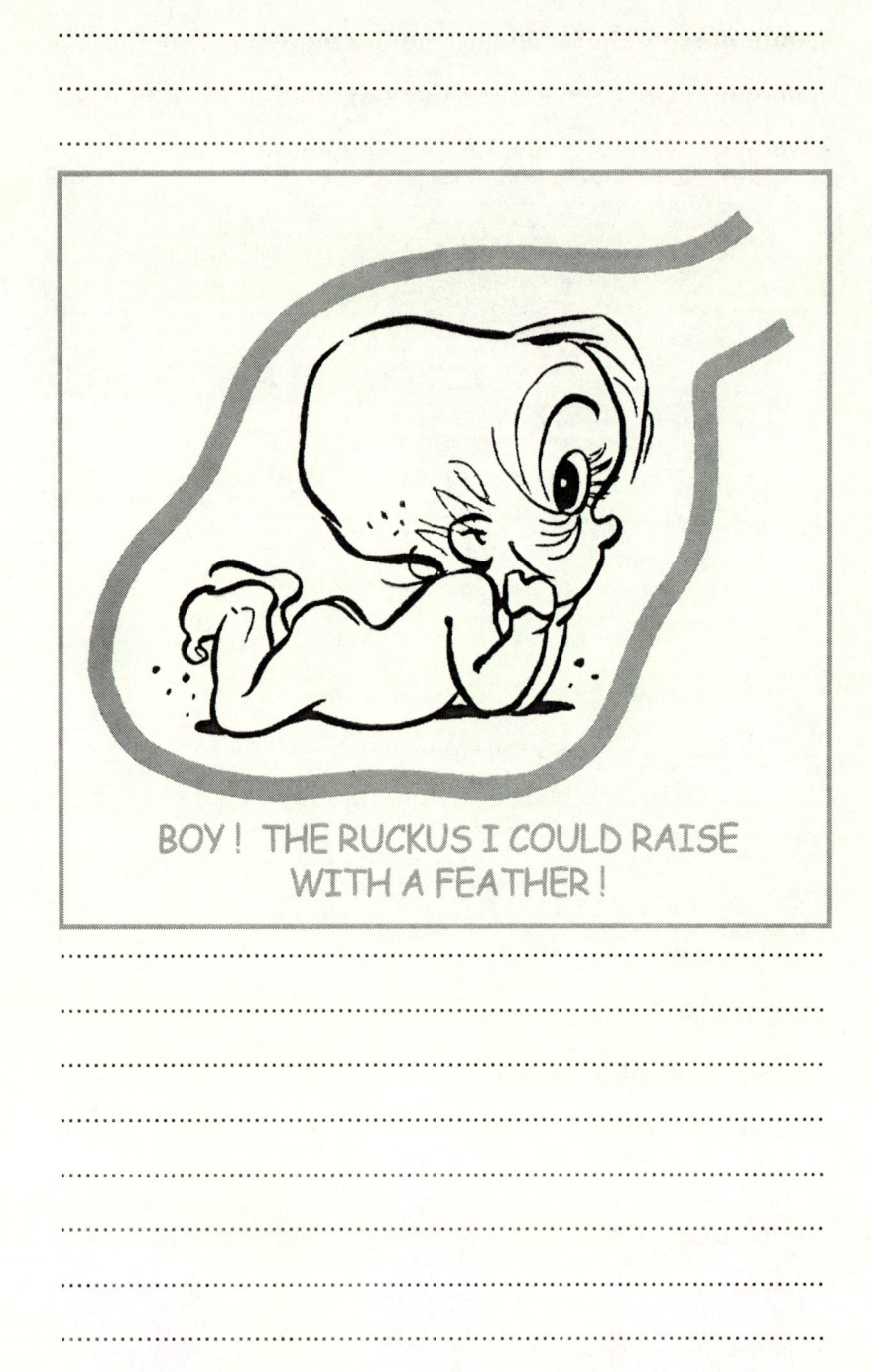

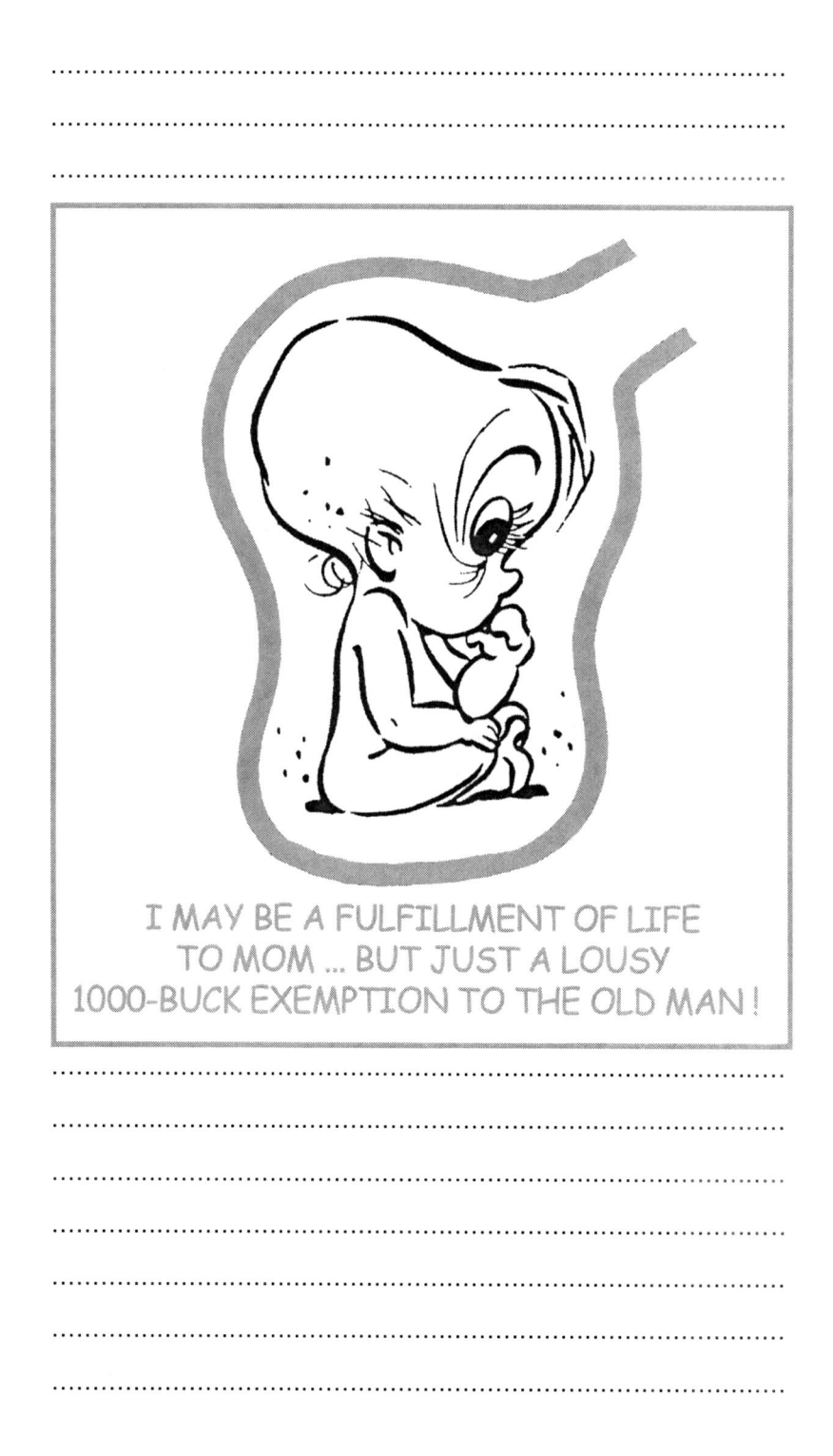

I MAY BE A FULFILLMENT OF LIFE TO MOM ... BUT JUST A LOUSY 1000-BUCK EXEMPTION TO THE OLD MAN!

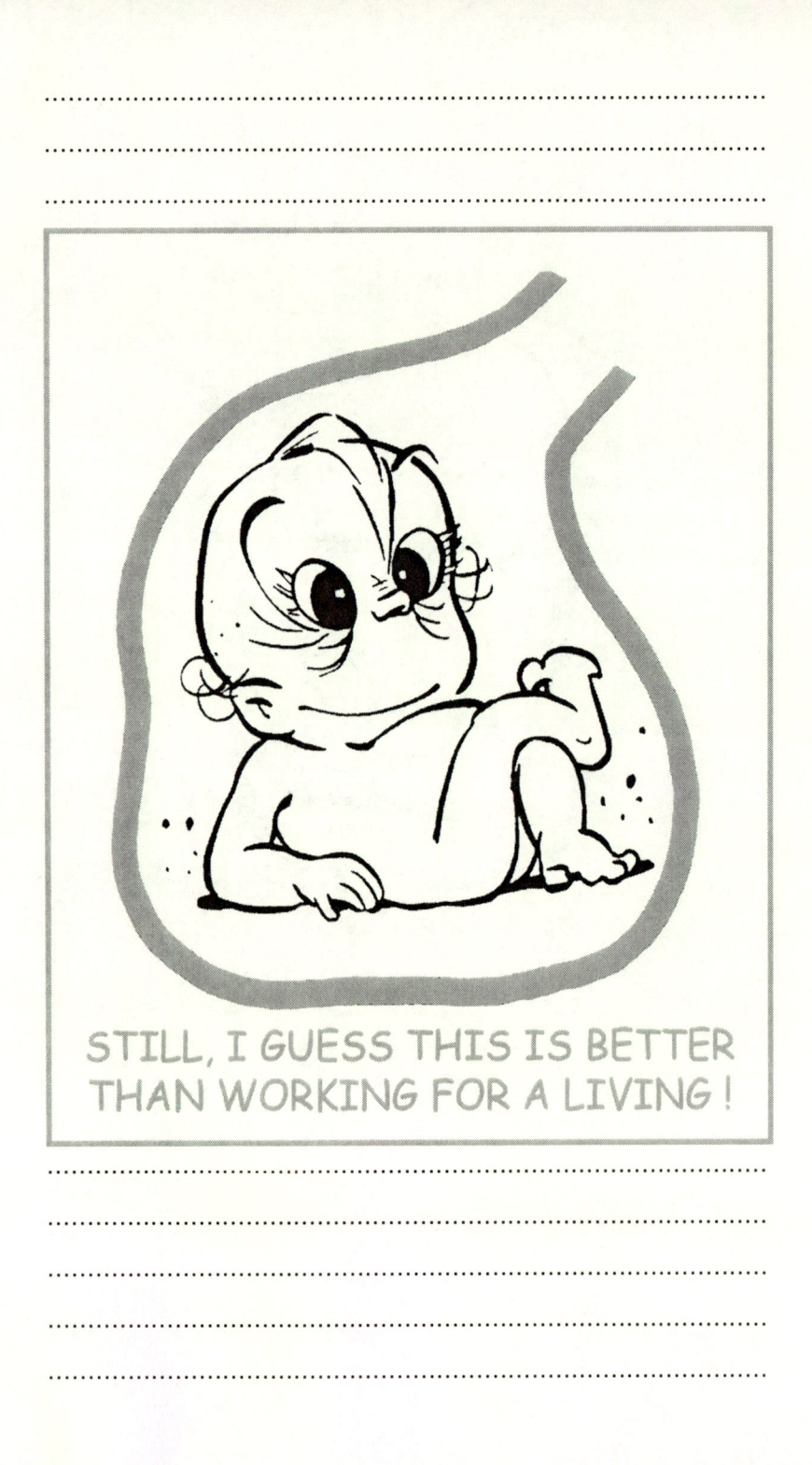

STILL, I GUESS THIS IS BETTER THAN WORKING FOR A LIVING!

Our First Ultrasound:

[paste ultrasound picture here]

WITH A LITTLE LIPSTICK AND EYE-SHADOW ... YOU'D MAKE A CUTE CHICK!

What We Could See:

....
....
....
....
....
....
....
....

What Your Pop Had to Say:

....
....
....
....

paste ultrasound picture here

....
....
....
....
....
....
....

WHAT A WAY TO SPEND CHRISTMAS!

MICHELLE'S GOT A NEW HAIR-DO ...
THE MARKET OPENED STRONG ...
AND ALL HELL'S BUSTED LOOSE
AGAIN IN THE MIDDLE EAST!

AW, SHUT UP! MY FOOT'S ASLEEP!

OH, ME MOTHER WAS A LADY ...

WHAT THE HELL'S GOTTEN INTO YOU ?

First Time I Felt You Move:

....
....
....
....
....
....
....
....
....

How I Felt:

....
....
....
....
....
....
....
....
....
....
....
....
....
....
....
....

MAN! SMELL THAT BACON!

I'M GONNA BE A STAR AND
I'M READY FOR MY CLOSE-UP!

C'MON, MOM ... BACK AWAY FROM THAT BARBEQUE!

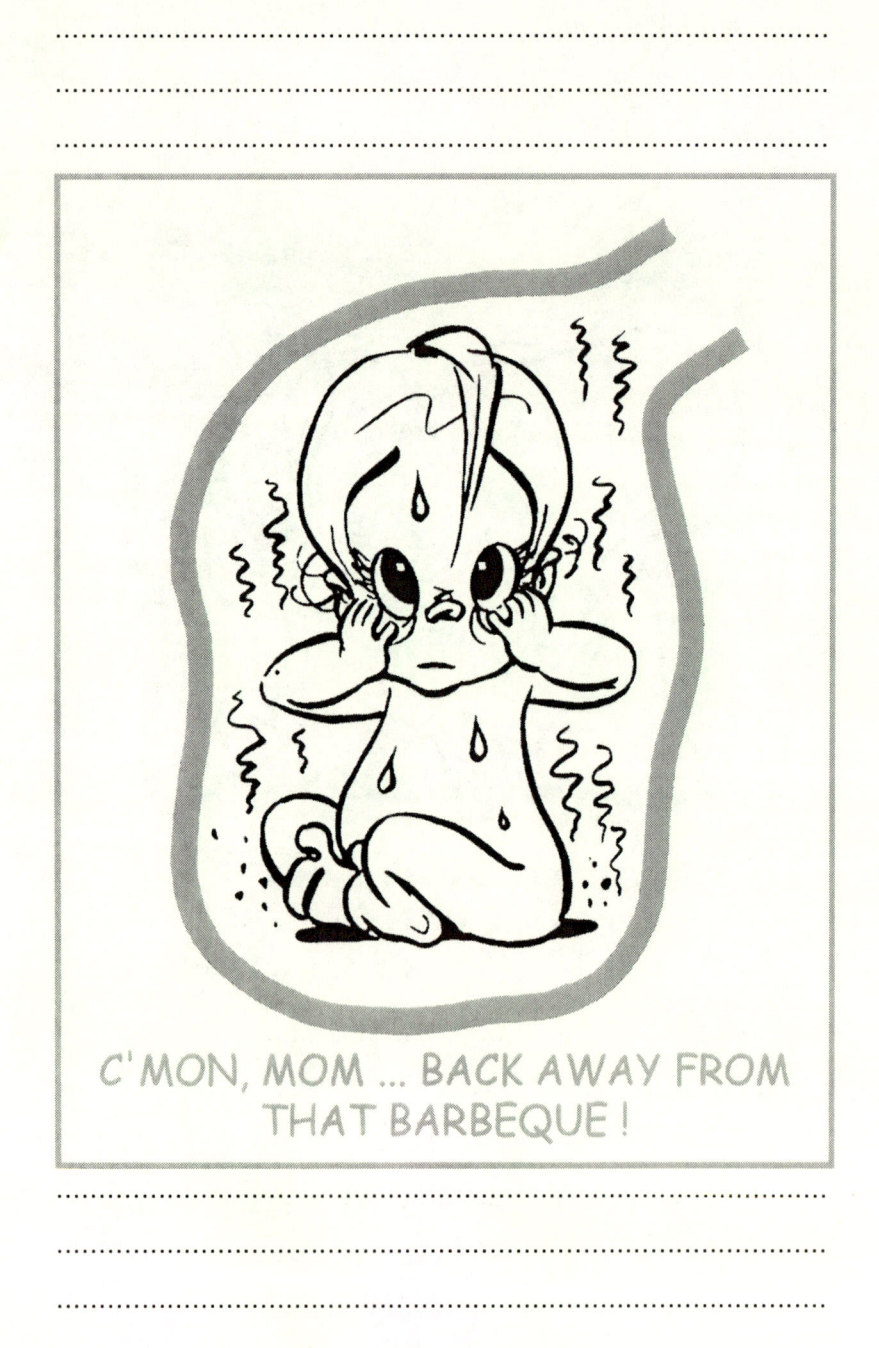

FIRST THING I DO WHEN I GET OUT IS WRING THAT EARLY-MORNING-CHIRPIN' PARAKEET'S NECK!

COME TO THINK OF IT ... I'M A PRETTY COMPLICATED LITTLE HUNK OF MACHINERY!

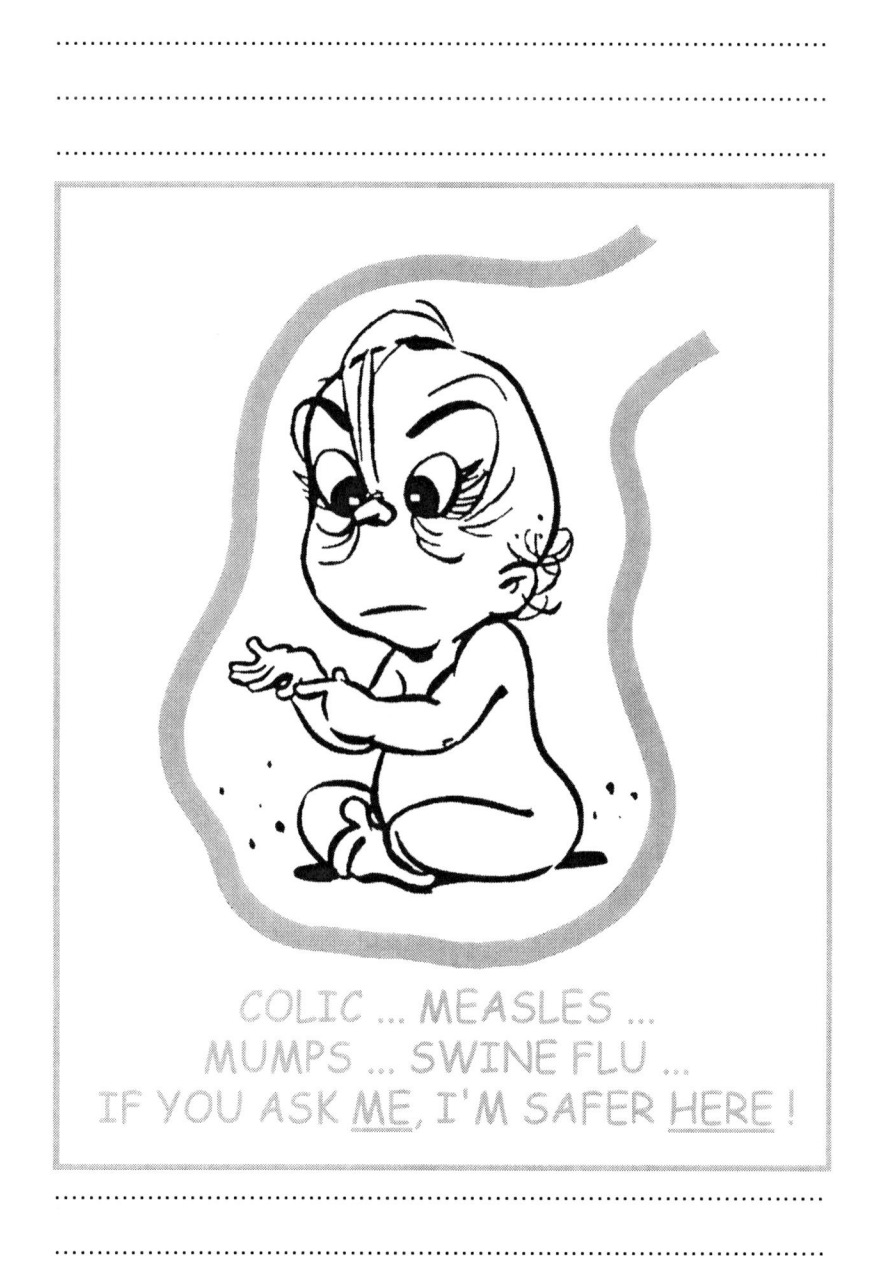

COLIC ... MEASLES ...
MUMPS ... SWINE FLU ...
IF YOU ASK ME, I'M SAFER HERE!

Special Memories:

....
....
....
....
....
....
....
....
....
....
....
....
....

Funny Memories:

....
....
....
....
....
....
....
....
....
....
....

HEY, MOM ... KNOCK ME OFF A LULLABY.
I CAN'T SLEEP!

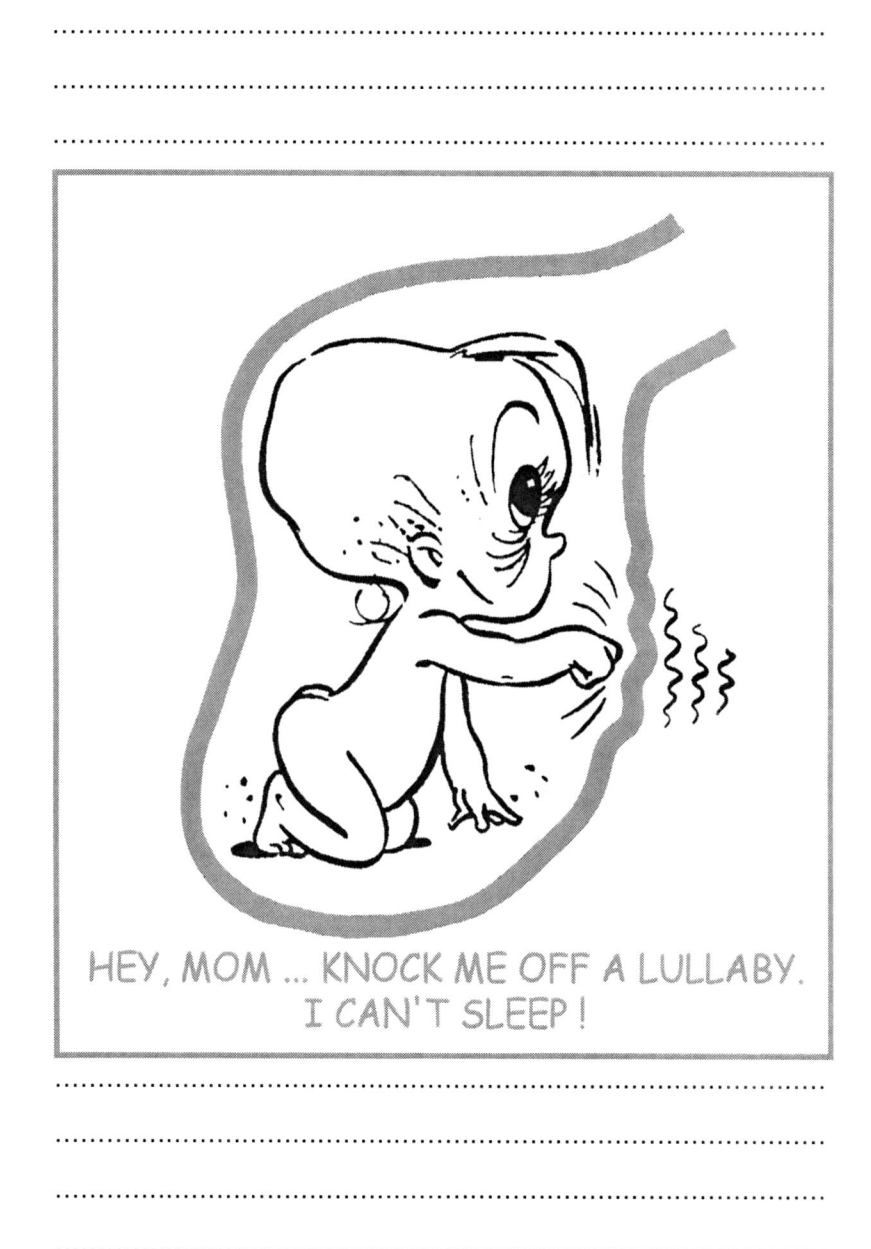

YOU'D THINK THE LITTLE PUNK'D WAIT UNTIL SHE'S <u>BORN</u> BEFORE SHE STARTS TEETHING!

ONE SOLID HOUR ON THE CELL-PHONE WITH THE DAMNDEST YAK I EVER HEARD!

I'VE BEEN IN HERE TOO LONG.
EVEN YOU LOOK GOOD TO ME.

... AND IF YOU THINK I'M RAISING A RUCKUS DOWN HERE ... WAIT 'TIL I GET OUTSIDE!

Do We Learn Your Sex or Wait to be Surprised:

....
....
....
....
....
....
....
....
....
....
....

What Your Pop Says:

....
....
....
....
....
....
....
....
....
....
....
....
....
....

GOWAN, LAUGH. BUT DON'T FORGET <u>YOU</u> COULD BE IN MOM'S FIX ANY MONTH NOW!

ZEESH! AND HE GETS PAID FOR THIS KIND OF AN EXAMINATION, TOO!

... AND TUNE THAT OUT OF YOUR STETHOSCOPE!

picture of me pregnant with YOU!

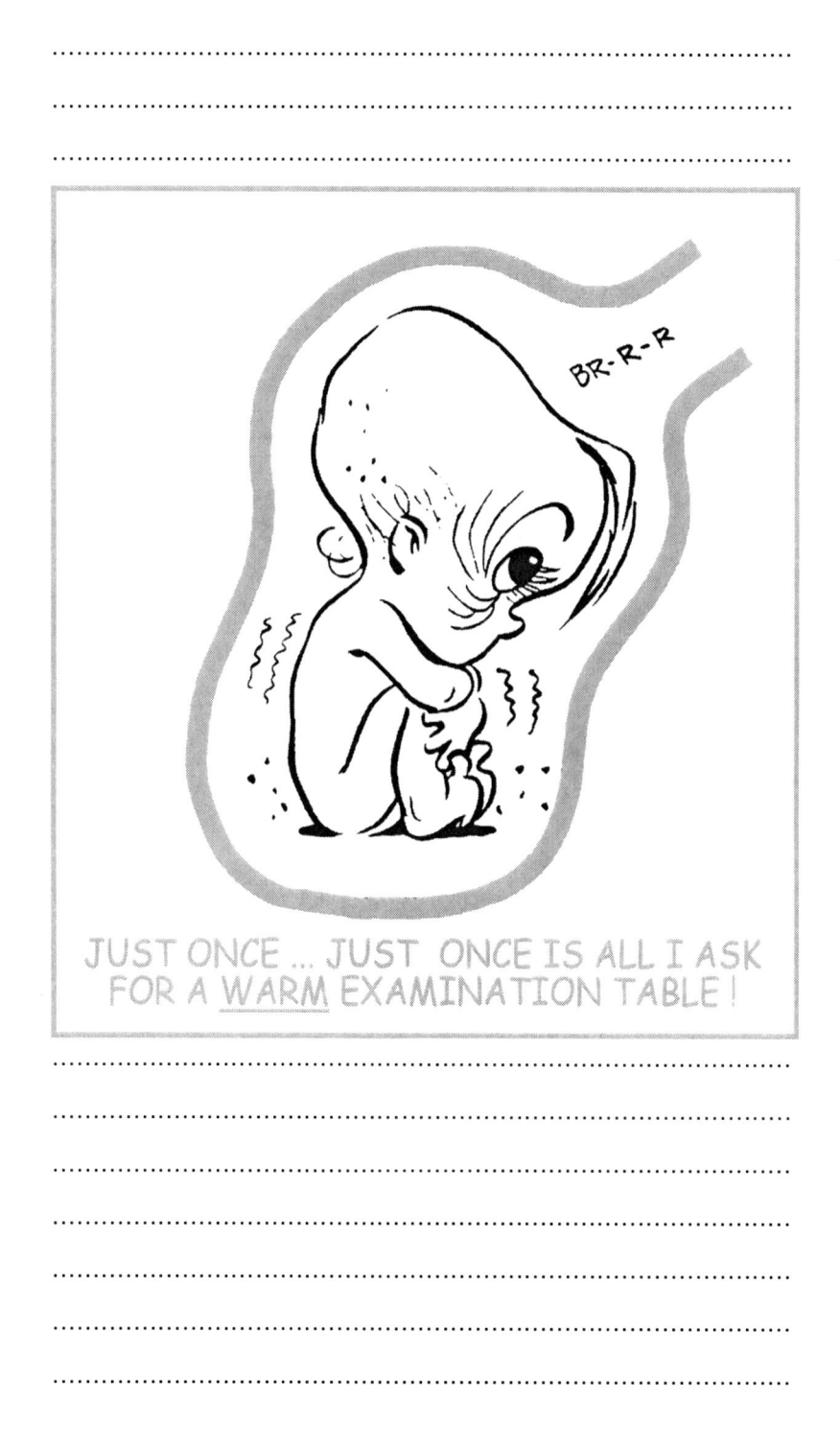

JUST ONCE... JUST ONCE IS ALL I ASK FOR A WARM EXAMINATION TABLE!

....
....
....

TODAY IT'S YOUR TURN TO LET DOC LISTEN TO YOUR HEART!

....
....
....
....
....
....
....
....

Hardest Things to Adjust To:

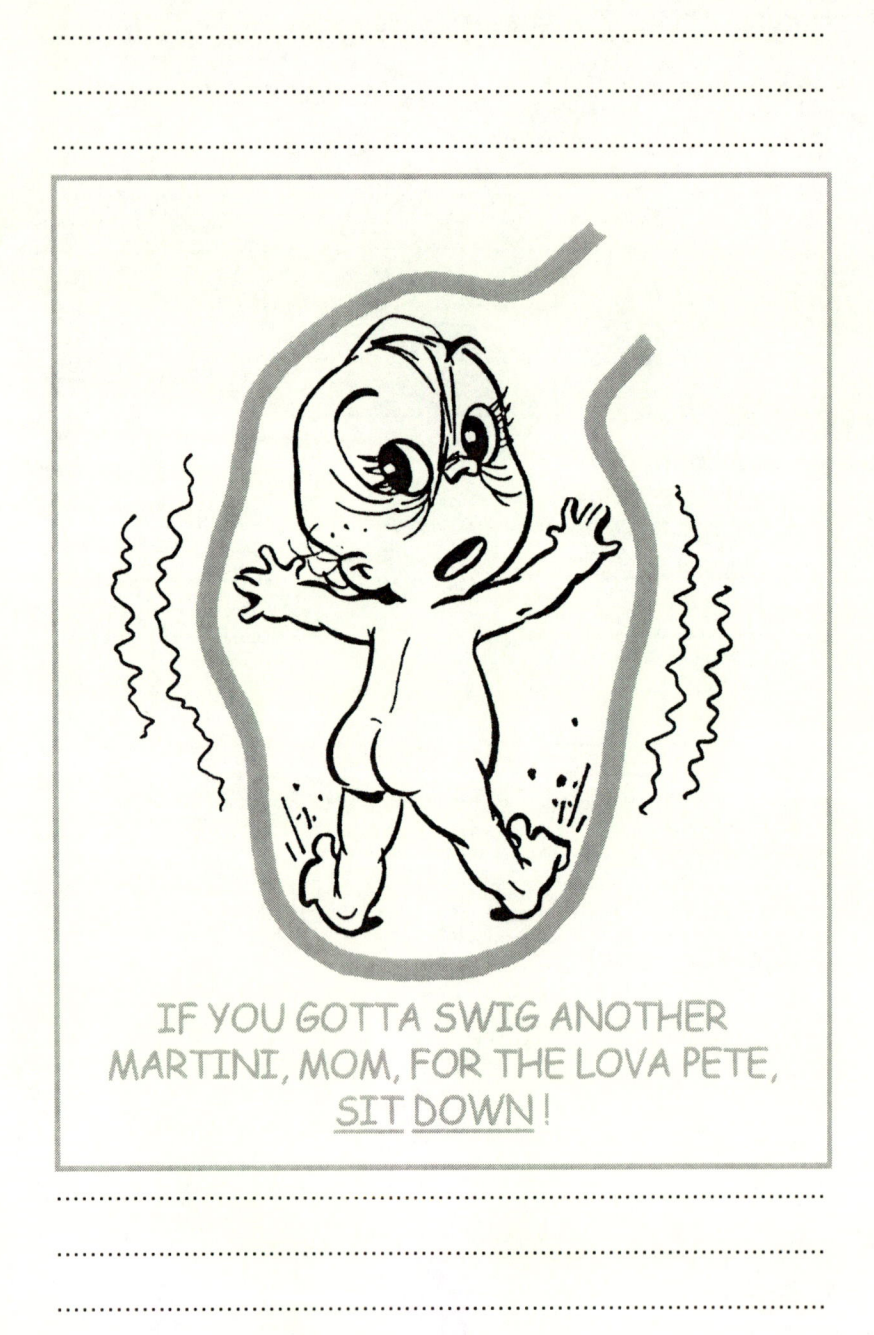

IF YOU GOTTA SWIG ANOTHER MARTINI, MOM, FOR THE LOVA PETE, <u>SIT DOWN</u>!

OH, MAN, ROAST CHICKEN! SHE'S AFTER SOMETHIN' FROM THE OLD MAN!

... AND IF YOU DON'T LIKE MY CHOICE OF LANGUAGE - GET THE HELL OUT!

Funny Moments:

....
....
....
....
....
....
....
....
....
....
....
....
....

Surprising Moments:

....
....
....
....
....
....
....
....
....
....
....
....
....
....

AW, C'MON POP, LAY OFF.
ME AND MOM HAD A HELLUVA DAY!

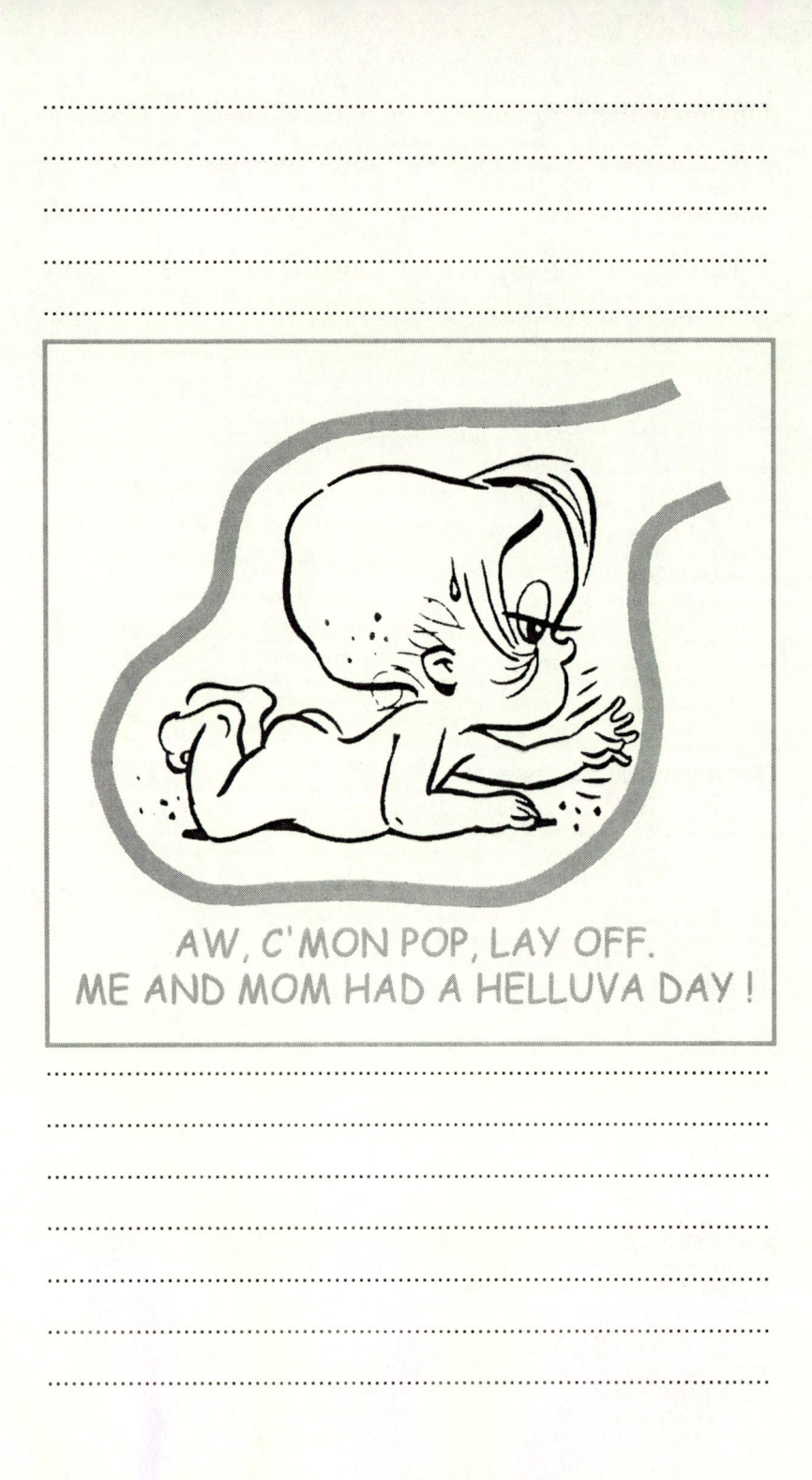

BOY! SHE SURE HAD FOLLOW-THROUGH ON <u>THAT</u> DRIVE!

WITH THOSE FANGS, YOU'RE A CINCH TO BE A BOTTLE-BABY!

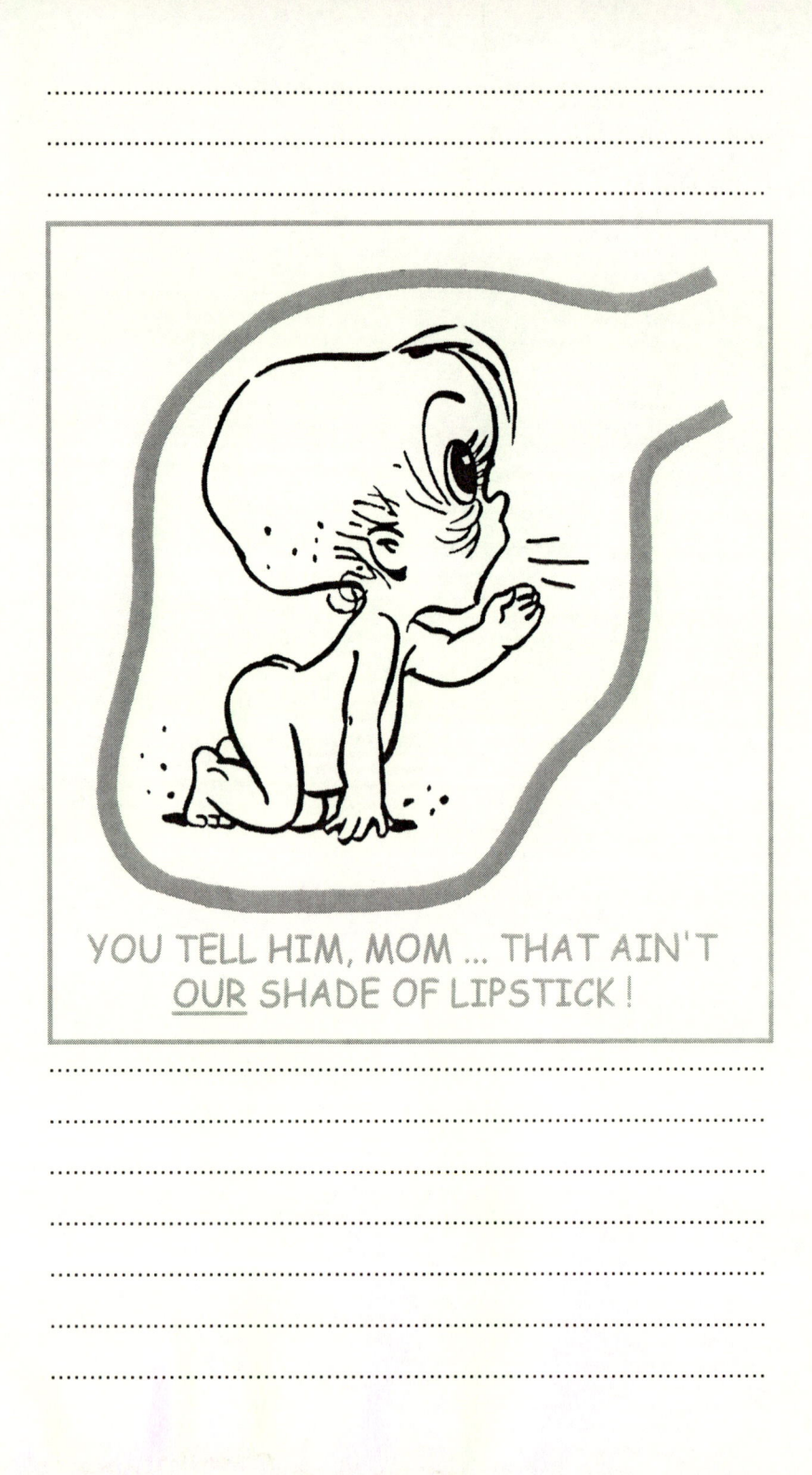

YOU TELL HIM, MOM ... THAT AIN'T <u>OUR</u> SHADE OF LIPSTICK!

What Your Pop Says:

....
....
....
....
....
....
....
....
....
....
....
....
....
....

picture of me pregnant with YOU!

....
....
....
....
....

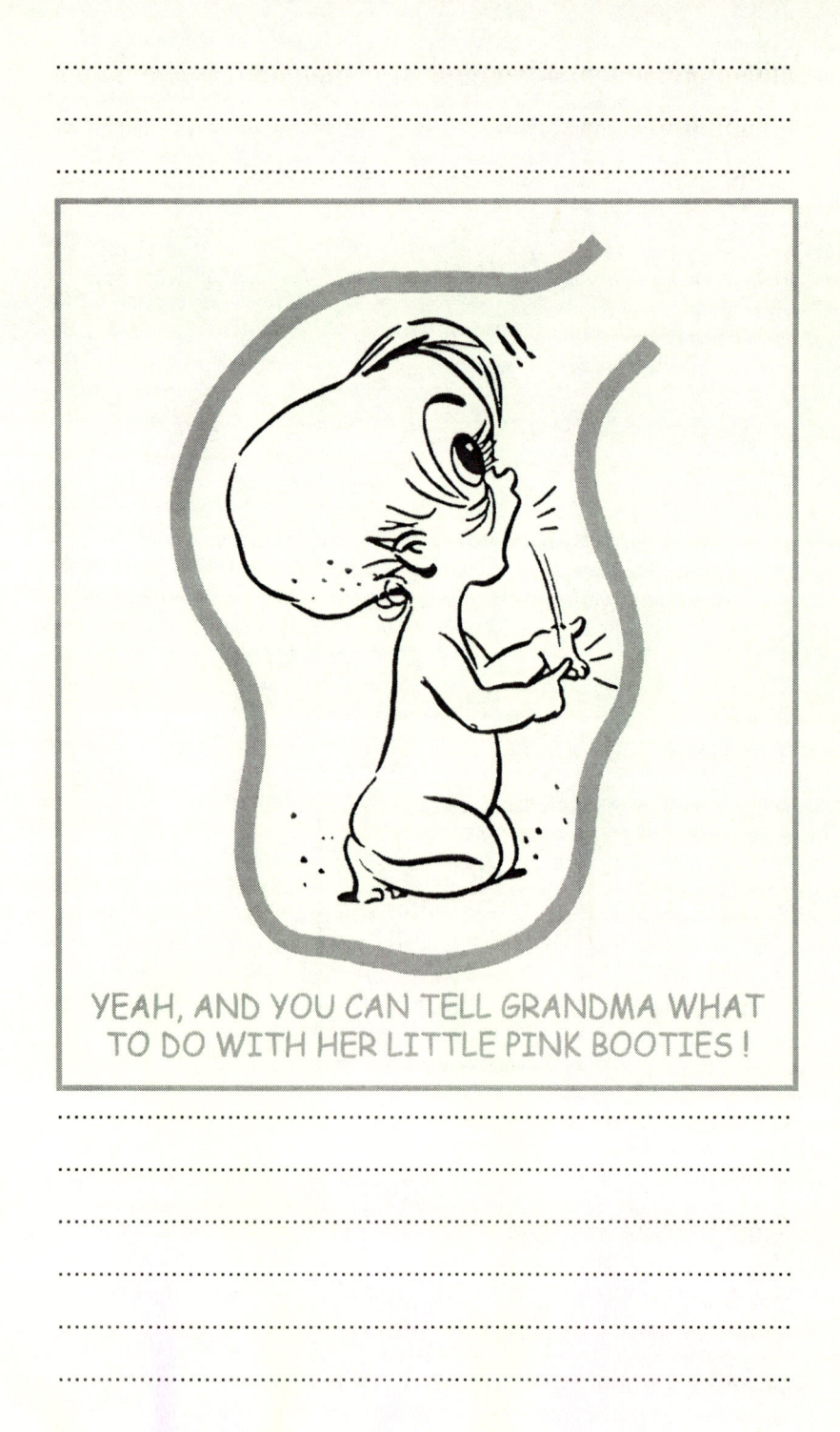

YEAH, AND YOU CAN TELL GRANDMA WHAT TO DO WITH HER LITTLE PINK BOOTIES!

WHATCHA WANT AT YOUR AGE, WATERMELONS, YET?

MA AND I SURE MUSTA
HUNG ONE ON LAST NIGHT!

Where's Your Nursery Going to Be:

....
....
....
....
....

Colors and Designs We Chose:

....
....
....
....
....
....
....
....

Special Gifts and Furniture:

....
....
....
....
....
....
....
....
....

I REALLY GOTTA TAKE CARE OF MYSELF TO KEEP THE FAMILY NAME GOIN'!

FOR A GIRL YOU SURE GOT A BONY BACK!

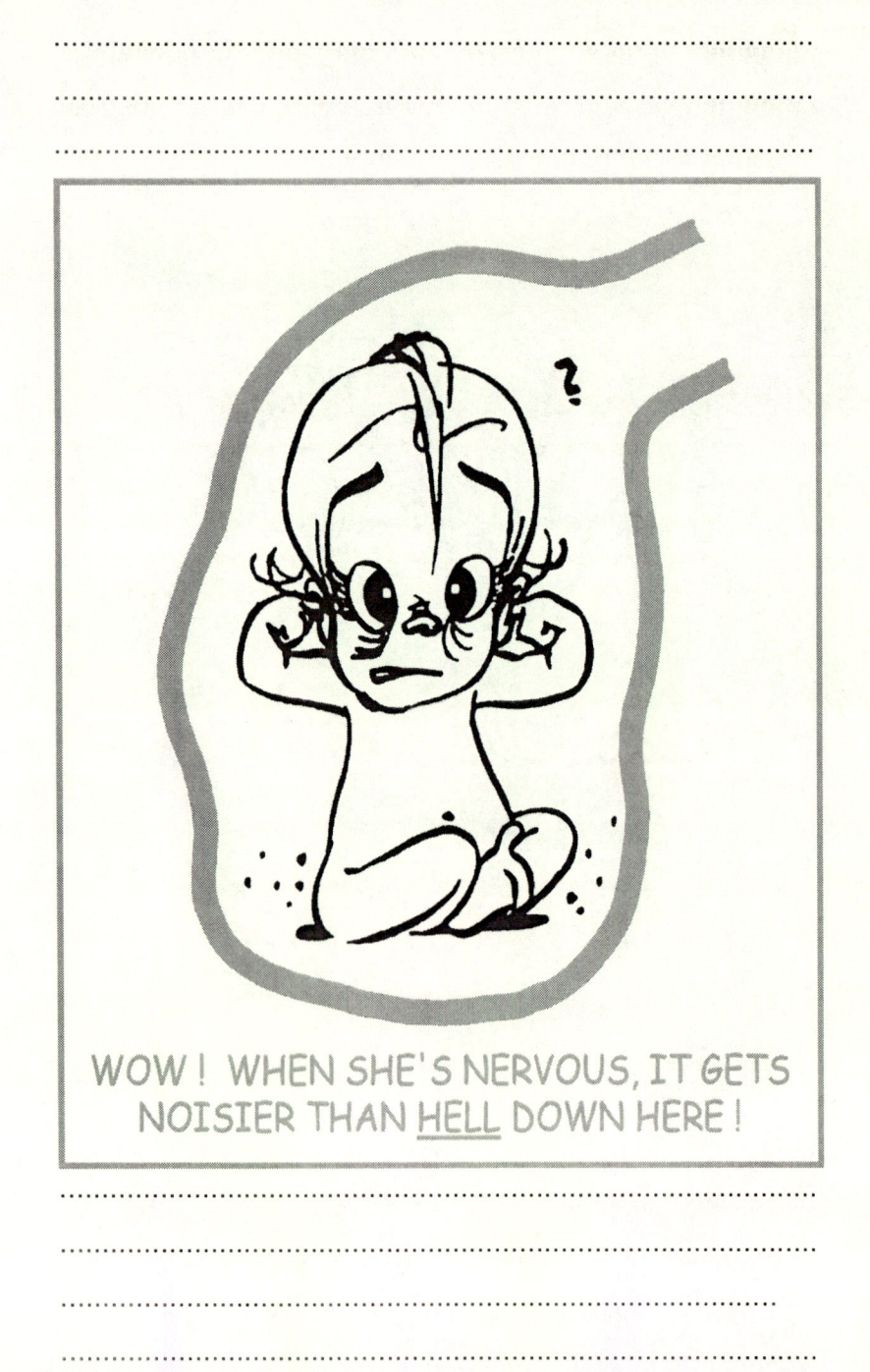

WOW! WHEN SHE'S NERVOUS, IT GETS NOISIER THAN <u>HELL</u> DOWN HERE!

I CAN SEE ME NOW. BEHIND THE WHEEL OF A FERRARI ... THE TOP DOWN AND A BLONDE CHICK IN THE OTHER BUCKET SEAT !

OH, COME OFF IT!

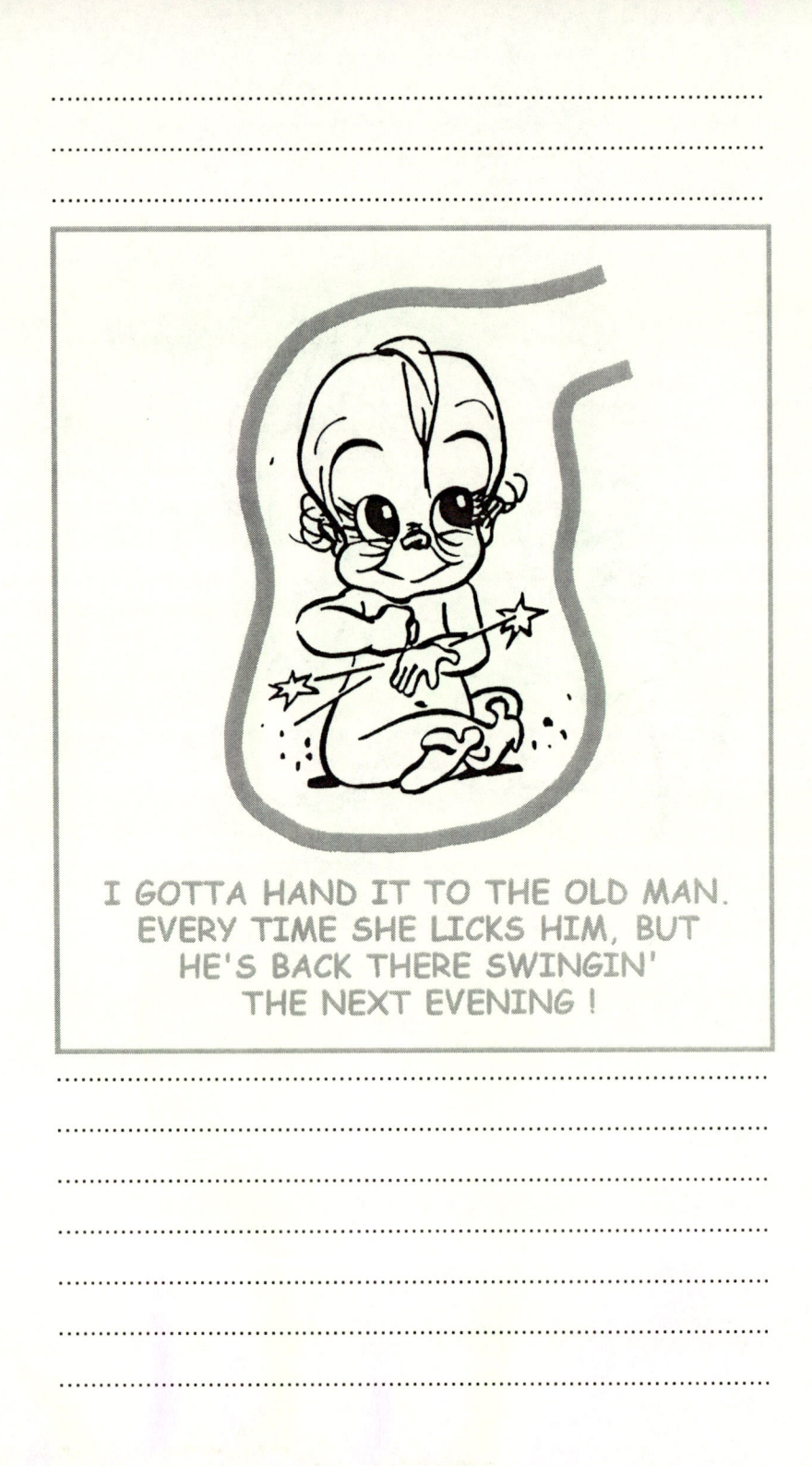

I GOTTA HAND IT TO THE OLD MAN.
EVERY TIME SHE LICKS HIM, BUT
HE'S BACK THERE SWINGIN'
THE NEXT EVENING!

... AND ANOTHER THING. NO EATIN' ANIMAL CRACKERS IN THE CRIB, SEE ?

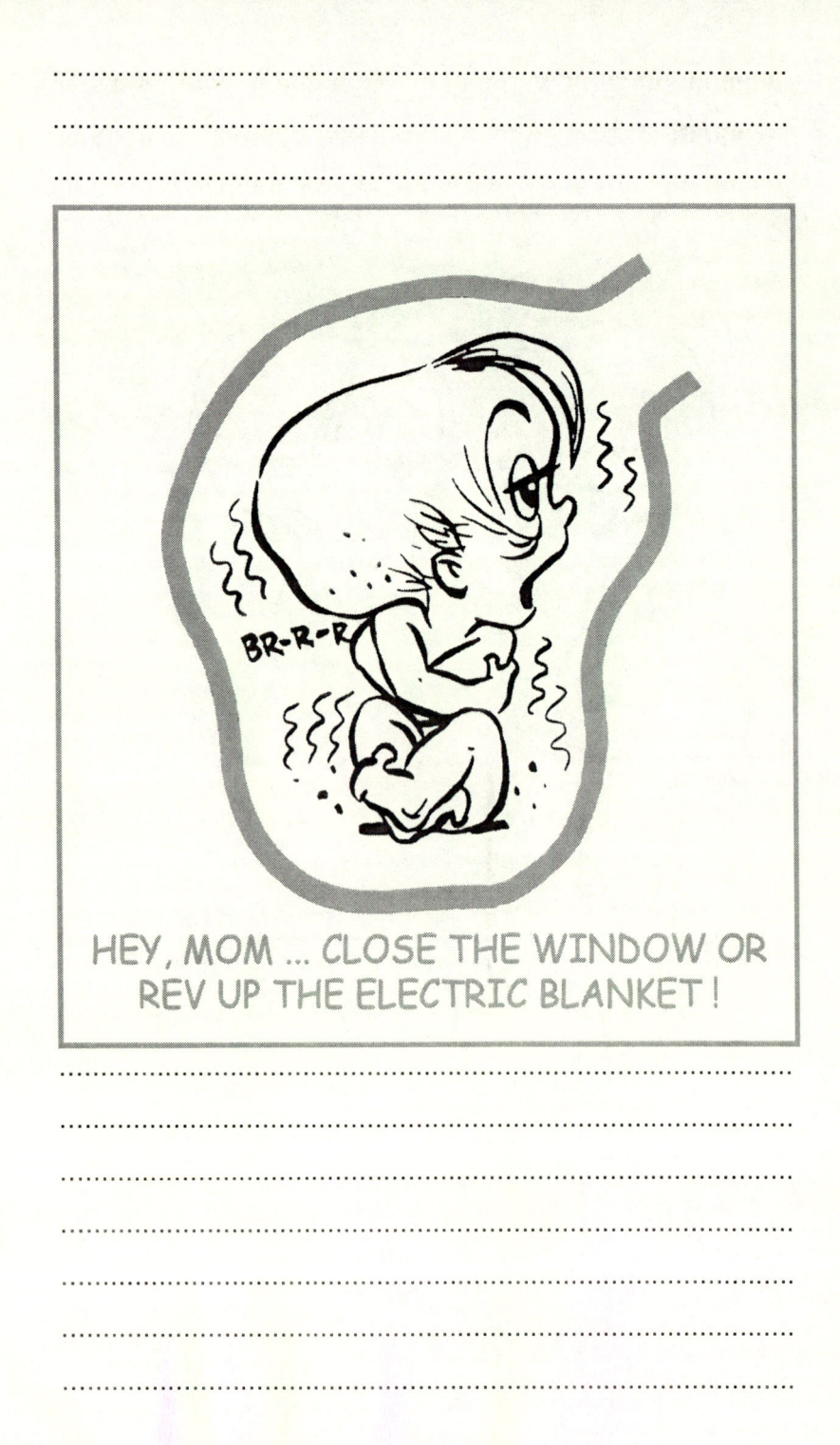

HEY, MOM ... CLOSE THE WINDOW OR REV UP THE ELECTRIC BLANKET!

Our First Baby Shower:

....
....
....
....
....

Who Was There:

....
....
....
....
....
....
....
....
....
....
....
....
....
....
....
....
....
....
....

IF HE WASN'T OUR POP, DO YOU THINK HE'D SHOW UP EVERY EVENING?

Gifts For You:

....
....
....
....
....
....
....
....
....
....
....
....
....
....
....
....

Gifts For Me:

....
....
....
....
....
....
....
....

BOY, ALL I'M GONNA DO THE FIRST WEEK IS S-T-R-E-T-C-H!

Funny Moments:

LAY OFF! WHO EVER HEARD OF GETTING BORN IN AN M.G.?

Special Moments:

....
....
....
....
....
....
....
....
....
....
....
....
....

[picture of me pregnant with YOU!]

....
....
....
....
....
....

JUST AS I THOUGHT. MOM'S GOT INDIGESTION AGAIN!

SAY IT AGAIN, DOC! ANY TIME NOW ... WOWIE!

YOU'RE DARN TOOTIN' MOM
AND I WANT A PRIVATE ROOM!

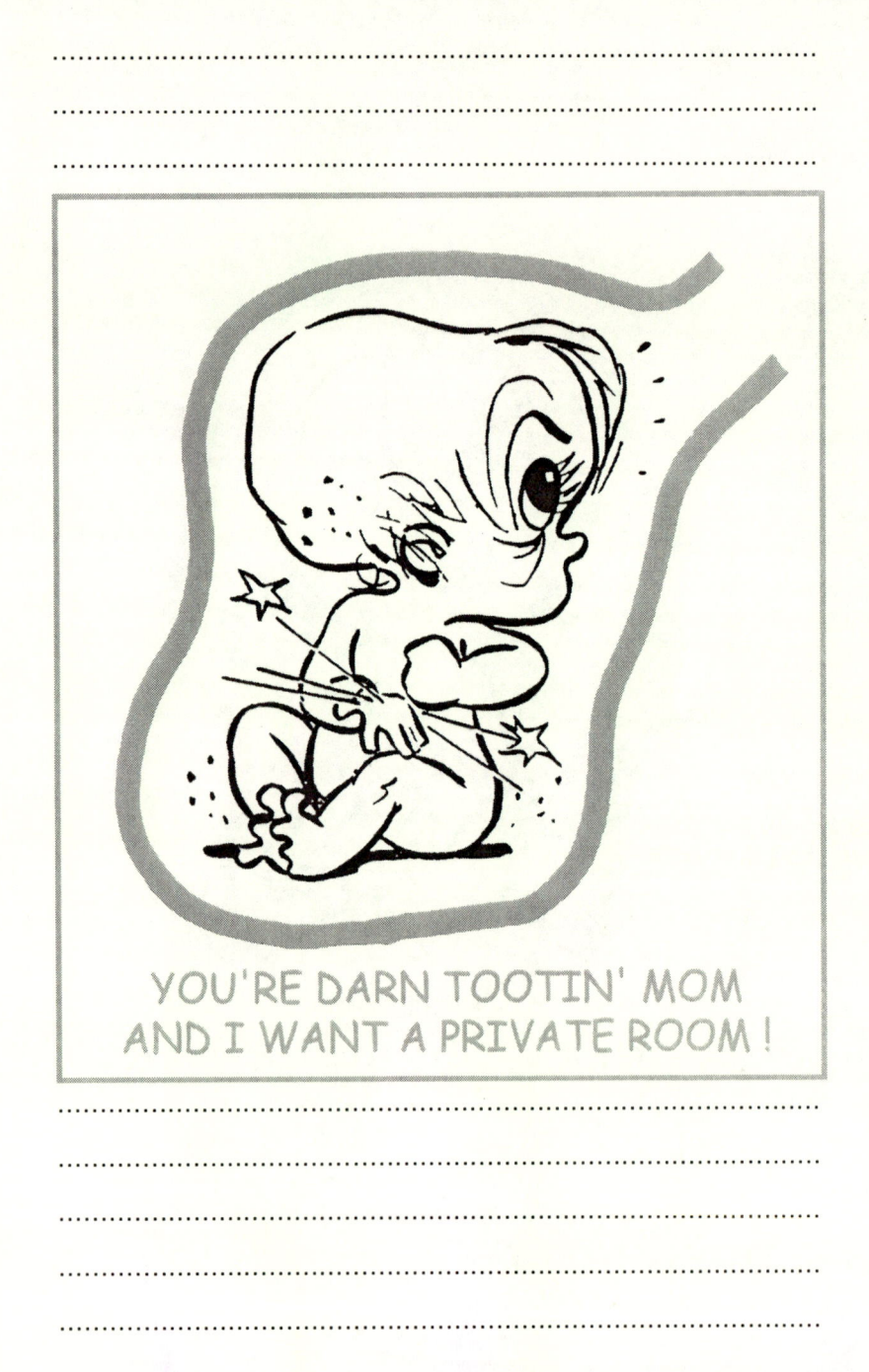

Names We Considered:

BOYS: GIRLS:

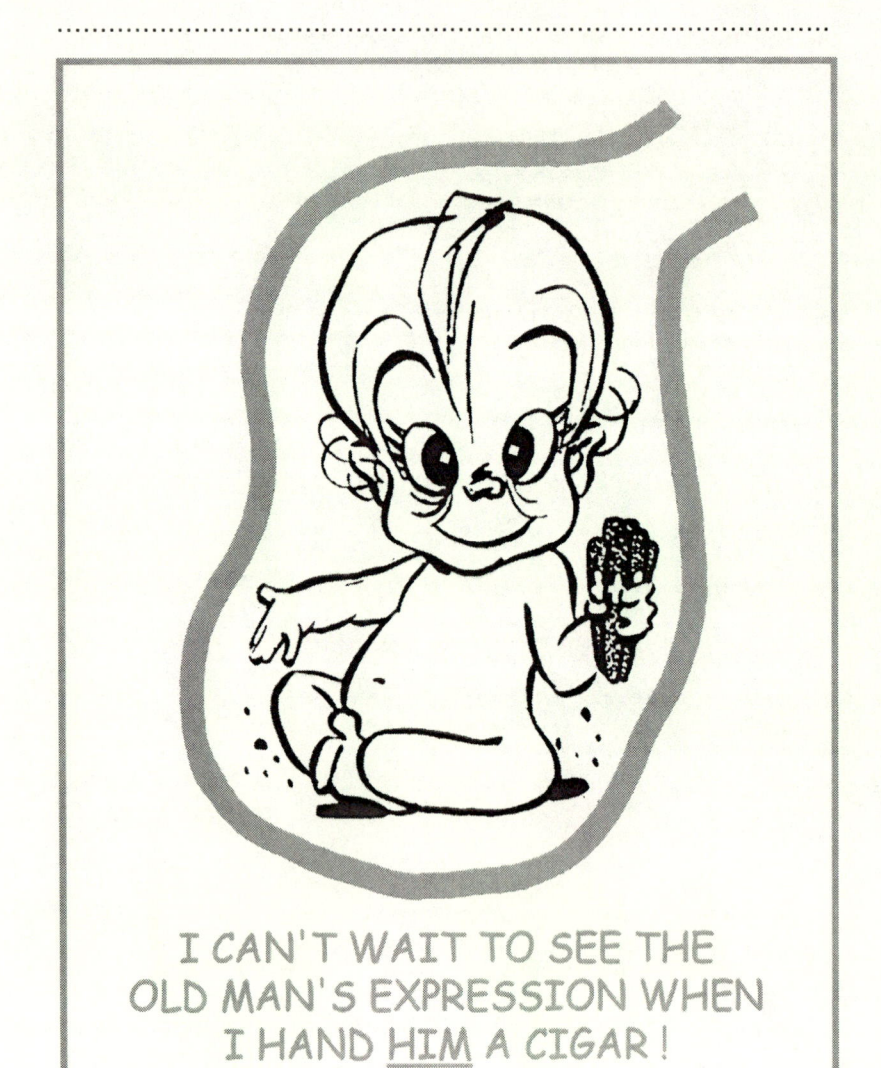

I CAN'T WAIT TO SEE THE OLD MAN'S EXPRESSION WHEN I HAND <u>HIM</u> A CIGAR!

Names We Finally Chose:

....
....
....
....
....
....

What The Names Mean:

....
....
....
....
....
....
....
....
....
....
....
....
....
....
....
....
....
....

WONDER IF SHE SAVVIES MORSE CODE?

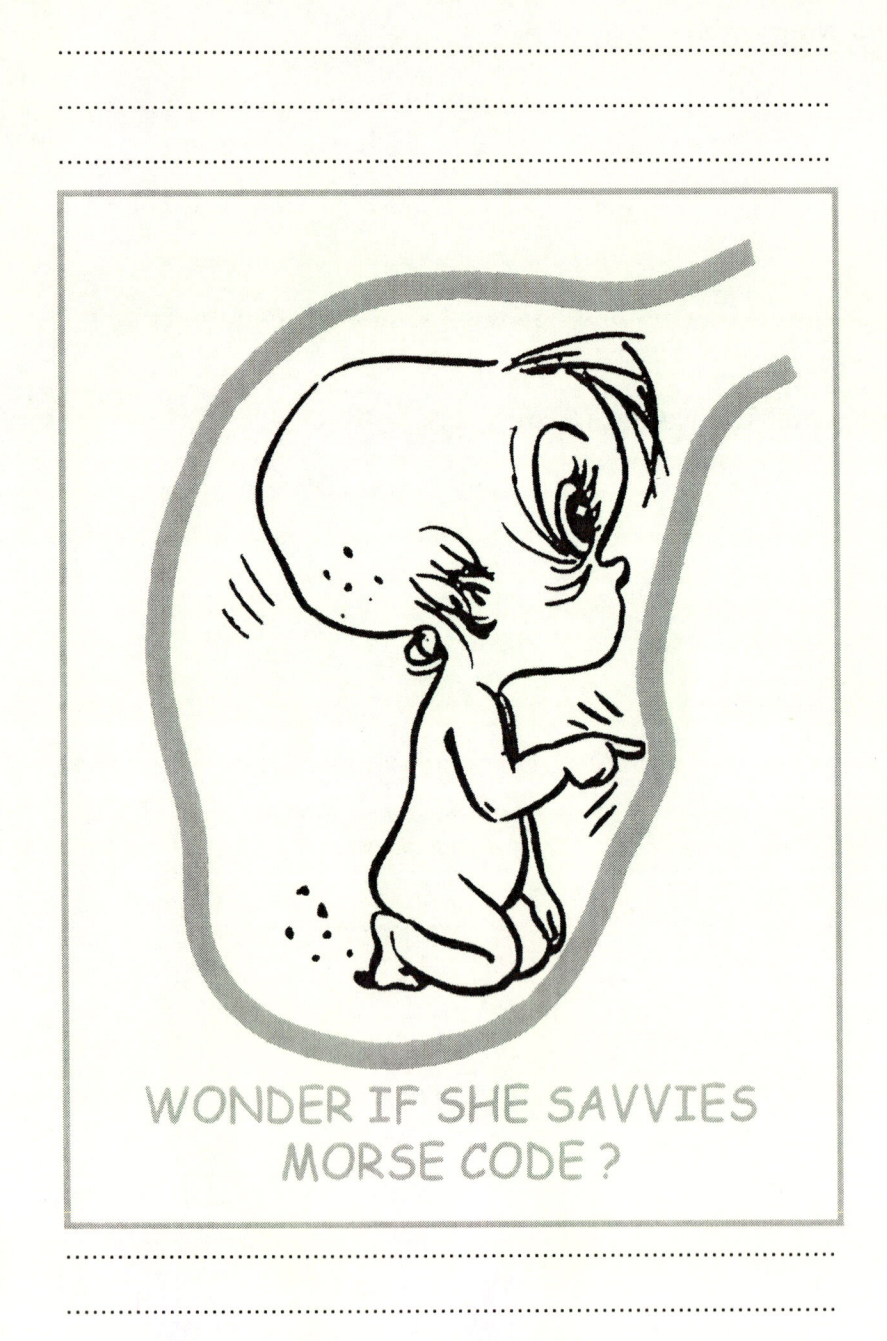

When We Know You Were Finally Coming:

....
....
....
....
....
....
....
....

What your Pop Did:

....
....
....
....
....
....
....
....
....
....
....
....
....
....
....
....

THEN I'LL SAY:
"YOU HAVEN'T FORGOTTEN
SOMETHING, HAVE YOU, DOC?"

Funny Memories:

....
....
....
....
....
....
....
....
....
....
....
....
....

Special Memories:

....
....
....
....
....
....
....
....
....
....
....
....
....

AW, DRY UP! YOU THINK SHE'S DOIN' THIS FOR A GAG?

You Were Born:

....

....

Where:

....

....

You Weighed:

....

You Were This Tall:

....

....

....

....

....

....

....

....

..............................┌──────────────────┐..............................
                              │   │
..............................│   Your   │..............................
                              │   first   │
..............................│   picture   │..............................
                              │   │
..............................└──────────────────┘..............................

....

....

....

....

CRIPES! SUPPOSE THEY DON'T LIKE ME?

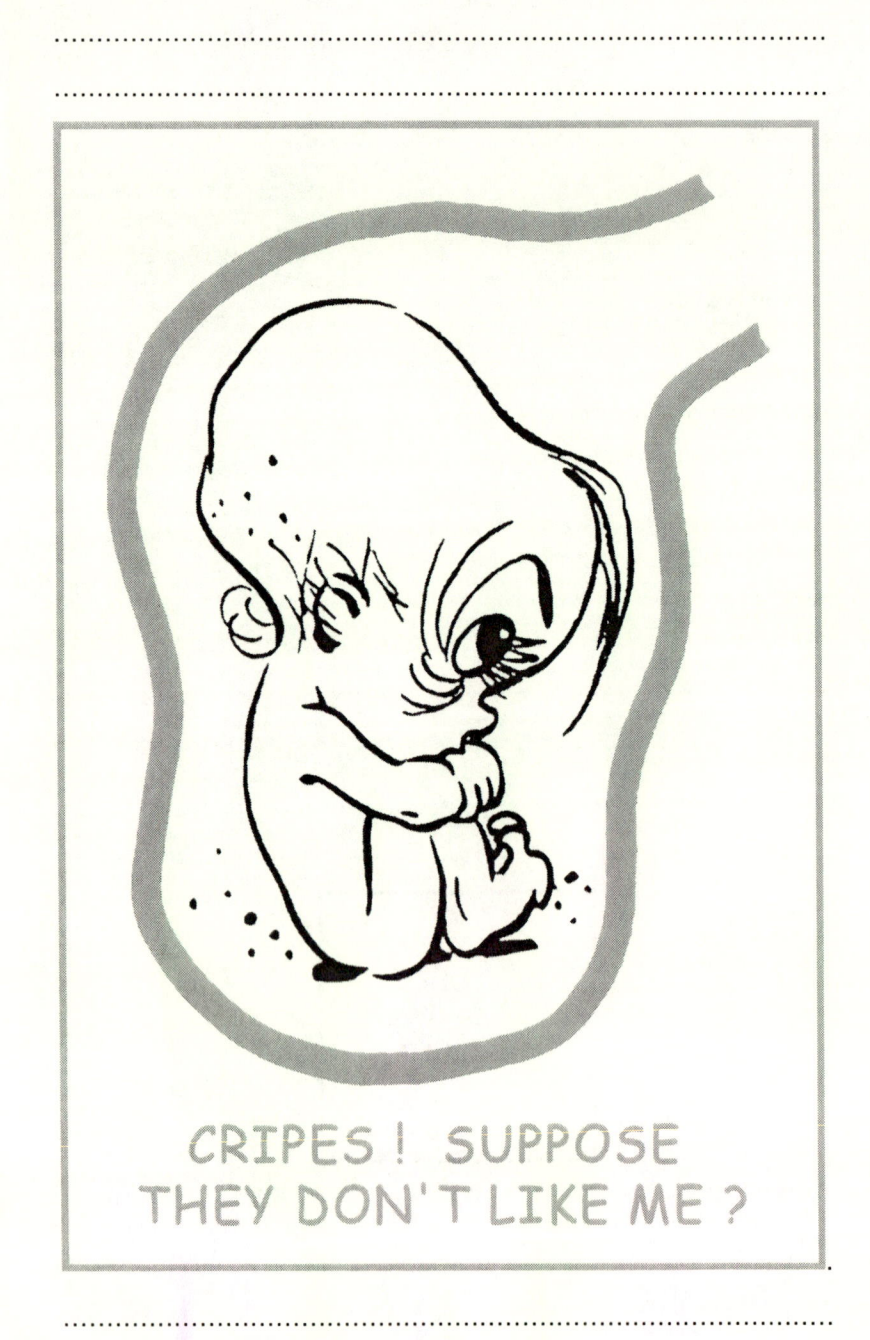

What your Pop Said:

....
....
....
....
....
....
....
....
....
....
....
....
....
....

Your First Visitors Were:

....
....
....
....
....
....
....
....
....
....
....

IF THINGS LOOK OKAY, I'LL WHISTLE YOU OUT!

Your First Night at Home:

....
....
....
....
....
....
....
....
....
....

┌─────────────────────────┐
│ First picture   │
│ of YOU and   │
│ Mommy & Daddy   │
└─────────────────────────┘

....
....
....
....
....
....
....
....

HEY! WHAT THE HELL'S THE RUSH!

```
............................................................
............................................................
............................................................
............................................................
............................................................
┌─────────────────┐
............│                 │...............
............│   Picture of    │...............
............│      YOU        │...............
............│    and Mom      │...............
............│                 │...............
............└─────────────────┘...............
............................................................
............................................................
............................................................
............................................................
............................................................
............................................................
............................................................
............................................................
............................................................
┌─────────────────┐
............│                 │...............
............│   Picture of    │...............
............│      YOU        │...............
............│    and Pop      │...............
............│                 │...............
............└─────────────────┘...............
............................................................
............................................................
............................................................
............................................................
```

Picture
of YOU
and
Mommy & Daddy

CPSIA information can be obtained
at www.ICGtesting.com
Printed in the USA
LVOW12s1235251117
557531LV00001B/84/P